Bad Girls from History

This is for my husband, Raymond, who passed away in December 2015 but was similarly intrigued by women who survive in history as unconventional, fascinating, or just downright evil.

Bad Girls from History

Wicked or Misunderstood?

Dee Gordon

PEN & SWORD
HISTORY

First published in Great Britain in 2017 by
Pen & Sword History
an imprint of
Pen & Sword Books Ltd
47 Church Street
Barnsley
South Yorkshire
S70 2AS

Copyright © Dee Gordon 2017

ISBN 978 1 47386 282 1

The right of Dee Gordon to be identified as the Author of this Work
has been asserted by her in accordance with the Copyright, Designs
and Patents Act 1988.

A CIP catalogue record for this book is available from the British
Library

Typeset in Ehrhardt by
Mac Style Ltd, Bridlington, East Yorkshire
Printed and bound in the UK by CPI Group (UK) Ltd,
Croydon, CR0 4YY

Pen & Sword Books Limited incorporates the imprints of Atlas,
Archaeology, Aviation, Discovery, Family History, Fiction, History,
Maritime, Military, Military Classics, Politics, Select, Transport,
True Crime, Air World, Frontline Publishing, Leo Cooper,
Remember When, Seaforth Publishing, The Praetorian Press,
Wharncliffe Local History, Wharncliffe Transport,
Wharncliffe True Crime and White Owl.

For a complete list of Pen & Sword titles please contact
PEN & SWORD BOOKS LIMITED
47 Church Street, Barnsley, South Yorkshire, S70 2AS, England
E-mail: enquiries@pen-and-sword.co.uk
Website: www.pen-and-sword.co.uk

Contents

Acknowledgements

It has been difficult to retain motivation during the illness and demise of my husband, so on this occasion my main thanks are directed at those friends who have kept me going in the absence of any family (my only son is autistic). So thanks to Donna and Steve Lowe, Denise Oanes, Laurel Padbury, Pat Stone, Debbi Campagna, Lisa Newman, Sandra Brown, Judith Williams, Kim Kimber, Peter Brown, Chris Sternshine, David Fox, Val Henderson and Diane Waterman. As for those assisting with research, this has mainly been staff at the British Library in London and at my local library in Southend on Sea especially Simon Wallace, who has since moved to Malta (and why not). Thanks also to everyone at Pen and Sword Books who have shown an interest and encouragement with regard to this project. Dependent on the feedback, there are enough women out there for a follow up!

Uncredited images are either in public domain, part of author's private collection, or sourced with relevant permissions via https://commons.wikimedia.org/ (If any credit has been misattributed or omitted, this will be corrected in any subsequent edition.)

Dee Gordon
www.deegordon-writer.com –
and an occasional contributor to Facebook

Introduction

Bad girls and wicked women – always a source of fascination. Especially fascinating is the why. Sometimes it is easy to arrive at the why, the motive: women prostituting themselves for money, or killing a husband for the love of a new man; desperate women stealing to survive, literally, or women from comfortable backgrounds who sought adventure or romance; women who were hungry for power or who were led astray by temptation.

One of the most difficult things to do when putting this book together was to choose from the many women in history that would qualify, so the choice is mainly down to providing variety for the reader. The other difficulty was in choosing which chapter to put them in – some killers could count as megalomaniacs, some courtesans as prostitutes, pirates as thieves, gangsters as killers, adulterers as exhibitionists. Certainly, a large percentage of the women featured earn their place in more than one chapter.

It has been difficult with the non-famous, mainly working class, individuals, to research their roots, assuming that such roots had an influence on their later lives and their reputations. And, if you are writing about 100 women rather than focusing on one, there are time constraints – it is very easy to spend a week searching the British Library Archives in London and end up with one relevant paragraph, though this also has something to do with being side-tracked by a fascinating, irrelevant, 'story'!

Note that some of the more obvious choices – e.g. Myra Hindley – are not included, mainly because they are just that; obvious. Enjoy the results of all this research and join in the author's love of and enthusiasm for the subject.

Chapter One

Courtesans and Mistresses

ARGYLL, Margaret, Duchess of 1912–93

Margaret, Duchess of Argyll.
(*Allan Warren*)

Even before becoming the third wife of the 11th Duke of Argyll in 1951, this society beauty was fuelling the gossip columns. The daughter of a Scottish millionaire, partly educated in New York, it was said that she lost her virginity at the age of fifteen to the actor David Niven. What is more well documented is her voracious sexual appetite and penchant for men of all ages and from the entire social strata. She had been engaged to the 7th Earl of Warwick, romanced by a Prince (Aly Khan), by the bisexual George, Duke of Kent – and by Lord Beaverbrook's son, Max Aitken; but it seems that there were also plenty of one night stands with whoever came her way! Her first marriage (1933–1947) was to Charles Sweeny, an American golfer, producing two children, and she had subsequent relationships with a Texas banker and the curator of the Metropolitan Museum of Art. A woman of eclectic tastes.

It was her taste for adultery and litigation that puts her into this book, however. When the Duke of Argyll sued for divorce in 1963, he introduced a list of eighty-eight men to the court, including government ministers and members of the royal family. The evidence was salacious enough to make all the national newspapers. There was her diary (apparently stolen by the duke) listing the physical attributes of her lovers, as if, according to the *Daily Telegraph*, she 'was running them at Newmarket'. First and foremost, however, there were the Polaroid photographs of the Duchess, wearing only three strings of pearls, fellating a man whose head is not in the photographs, and who has therefore never been identified with certainty. Possibly the actor Douglas Fairbanks Junior? Or Duncan Sandys, Winston Churchill's son in law? Perhaps even the Duke of Edinburgh? The general consensus favoured Douglas Fairbanks, but the (also controversial) Lady Colin Campbell, the Duchess's step-daughter-in-law, has gone on record as stating that the man was Pan Am executive Bill Lyons … the Duchess herself never revealed the truth, even in her 1975 memoirs *Forget Me Not*.

The court case lasted eleven days, with the judge summing up the Duchess as 'a completely promiscuous woman … wholly immoral'. Not unexpectedly, the Duke was granted his divorce, following a judgment that ran to a near novel-length 40,000-plus words, one of the longest in history. The case itself probably cost the Duchess more than £200,000 but it didn't stop her suing, in the ensuing years, her daughter, her landlord, her bank, her stepmother, and her servants, usually for libel and usually unsuccessfully. The 1970s were full of lavish parties but she was forced, financially, to sell her house in Upper Grosvenor Street in 1978, and took up residence in Grosvenor House, from where she was finally evicted over unpaid rent in 1990, ending up in a nursing home in Pimlico.

The Duchess had been Deb of the Year and one of the Top Ten Best Dressed Women in the World. She had also, as Mrs Sweeny, been immortalised in the words of the Cole Porter song 'You're The Top' – he rhymed her with 'You're Mussolini'… and it is Mr Sweeny who is her companion in death, at Brookside Cemetery, Woking.

BELLANGER, Marguerite 1840–86

There are enough notorious French courtesans to fill a book and indeed, French libraries are full of such books. Marguerite Bellanger was a little different, hence her inclusion here. A farm girl, a bit of a tomboy, outspoken, an unsuccessful actress with thick ankles … but Napoleon III, who met her in a park in Vichy in 1863, when she was twenty-three, was attracted by her blonde hair, black eyes, and vivacious personality. It seems they met in the rain, but stories of the meeting vary enormously: she was sheltering; he was sheltering; she offered him a raincoat; he offered her a rug; he was hunting;

she was riding … but meet they did and the attraction was obviously instant.

Born Julie Leboeuf, her surname gave rise to unappealing nicknames, hence her change of name once she had escaped from her life of poverty as a laundress. She became a dancer and bare-back horsewoman at a provincial circus, seduced along the way by a handsome lieutenant, until ending up on the stage before she was twenty. But she was not keen on criticism from the Paris audiences, and started on the road to prostitution (sometimes described as a 'second rank cocodette') attracting the French C list, for instance, the son-in-law of the President.

The Emperor Napoleon III was of course the supreme catch. She was his last mistress (1863–1865) and said to be his favourite, until she wanted too much influence and

Marguerite Bellanger, a bust sculpted by Albert-Ernest Carrier-Belleuse at the Musee Carnavalet, Paris.

spent too much money (such as buying two horses for 25,000 francs), becoming something of an embarrassment. The Empress Eugenie, who had tolerated Napoleon's previous mistresses, was less tolerant of Marguerite and apparently confronted her, telling her that she was 'killing' the Emperor, not that this made any difference.

In 1864, Marguerite had a son, Charles, without naming the father. She may well have falsified the date of his birth to make him more likely to be Napoleon's son. Regardless of this theory, Napoleon, in his mid-fifties, rather generously, looked after the boy financially, settling property on him as well as on Marguerite. However, once the affair was over, she sold a hotel he had bought for her, keeping some of the land, and a chateau, to ensure she could maintain status and lifestyle. After more, less high profile, liaisons, she went on to marry a Prussian officer in the British Army, William Kulbach, gaining respectability in her thirties. Her 'confessions' were published in 1882 and her memoirs, posthumously, in 1890, but neither were salacious enough to be successful. She is said, however, to have provided the career that inspired Emile Zola's best-selling *Nana*, published in 1880.

CLARKE, Mary Anne c.1776–1852

Here we have that classic example of an ambitious actress who found it more profitable to be the mistress of an influential royal. From lowly origins in London, by around 1803 she was entertaining the glitterati of London with the help of twenty servants and three cooks, drinking from wine glasses costing a remarkable two guineas each.

Mary Anne Clarke, from an illustration by Chas. Keene in *Our People*, Bradbury and Agnew, 1881.

Details of Mary Anne's parentage and early life are unclear (although her descendant, Daphne Du Maurier, wrote of her as having East London roots) but she certainly married the young, attractive Joseph Clarke in 1794, whom she had apparently met when he was a lodger at her family home. At the time of their marriage, Mary Anne, not yet eighteen, was establishing herself as an actress, playing roles at such popular venues as the Haymarket Theatre in London's West End. But Joseph, the proprietor of a stone-masonry business, seemed to offer the cultured and rich antecedents Mary Anne craved. Things did not work out as planned, however, because Joseph liked spending money and ended up bankrupt.

Two children later, she left him, with her profession giving her access to a number of subsequent liaisons culminating in a relationship with Frederick Augustus, Duke of York, a probable member of Mary Anne's smitten audience. It seems that Mary Anne had been promised over £1000 a year by the Duke in addition to the elegant London home and all its trappings, but this allowance was not paid regularly, her resultant debts necessitating a boost to her income. There were always those seeking promotion – military, civil, even clerical, and Mary Anne was happy to take money from them in return for her influence.

Her affair with the Duke turned into a political scandal in 1809, when he was charged with corruption as a result of her activities. The principal witness for the prosecution was listed as: 'Mary Anne Clarke of Loughton Lodge in the County of Essex, a widow' although it is not clear whether in fact Joseph was dead. In spite of the way the Duke had shaken her off, exposed her to poverty and infamy and refused her a promised annuity, all damning in the eyes of his public persona, the Duke was acquitted on the charges of corruption. The scandal was the Watergate of Regency London with major coverage in every newspaper.

His ex-mistress's subsequent threat to publish her memoirs – to pay for her children's future – resulted in the Duke's resignation as Commander-in-Chief of the Army and in a legal agreement being drawn up between Mary Anne and her former lover. He agreed that she would receive more than £7,000 (diverse amounts were recorded), a generous annuity for life, and two hundred pounds for each of her children. Blackmail? Some would say so. Adept political manoeuvring would be another interpretation.

Mary Anne could not lay down her pen and libellous publications continued, resulting in her spending nine months in Marshalsea Prison. The only bright spot during this period was the commissioning of her son, George, to the 17th Light Dragoons, thanks to a promise made long ago by the Duke which she had not expected to materialise.

After her release, she was *persona non grata*. She lived in France for a number of years, in constrained but fashionable conditions and died alone in Boulogne in 1852, her death reported in *The Times* by the Paris correspondent.

Postscript: While the Grand Old Duke of York had a nursery rhyme dedicated to him ('He had ten thousand men' etc …) a rhyme associated with Mary's downfall is less well known:

'Mary Anne, Mary Anne, Cook the slut in a frying pan' (!)

CLEOPATRA 68 BC–30 BC

Perhaps the most famous femme fatale of all, what is known about this fascinating woman is culled from what other people wrote about her; Plutarch, or Julius Caesar's own works. She was one of the last members of the Ptolemaic dynasty with its roots in incest, treachery and murder. Her father left the kingdom of Egypt to Cleopatra (then seventeen) and his elder son, Ptolemy XIV (eleven) who began their joint reign in 51 BC but who became extremely competitive, both wanting to rule Egypt.

Cleopatra, as portrayed by Frederick Sandys in *Cornhill Magazine*, Vol xiv, 19th century

When Caesar and his Roman army arrived in Egypt, Cleopatra's brother had already had Caesar's rival for the throne, Pompey, murdered, which hadn't pleased Caesar as much as expected. Cleopatra realised that she was more likely to charm him than defeat him and had herself 'delivered' to him rolled up in bedding – pleasing him with her initiative, but upsetting Ptolemy who saw her secretive arrival as a betrayal. He was to drown when attempting withdrawal from the Romans, with other Egyptians, following a battle on the banks of the Nile.

While not as beautiful as Elizabeth Taylor, Cleopatra certainly had the personality, sensuality and 'sweetness' to successfully woo such a womaniser as Caesar, a man in his fifties, and their affair resulted in a pregnancy, keeping Caesar in Egypt for much longer than planned.

Legally and traditionally, Cleopatra was now Queen and had married Ptolemy in keeping with Egyptian custom. But Caesar had to take up his neglected duties, leaving three Roman legions behind to protect her. When Cleopatra arrived in Rome to join him in 45 BC, accompanied by her 'husband' and young son, the splendour of her arrival amazed even the wealthy Romans. The Romans, however, and perhaps hypocritically, were not fond of this foreigner, this public flaunting of Caesar's mistress. In the meantime, her brother-husband vanished … very conveniently.

Cleopatra was left with no protection once Caesar was assassinated in 44 BC and she returned to rule Egypt with her son Ptolemy XVI, the last of his dynasty. Another, younger, Roman, Mark Antony, requested a meeting in Ephesus – in what is now Turkey – and was treated to another of Cleopatra's magnificent arrivals, on a suitably bedecked barge. He too became enamoured with the manipulative queen, even though she persuaded him to have her sister, a threat to her power, assassinated. He could refuse her nothing it seems. The duo produced three children, and, when his wife died, his idea of marrying his rival Octavian's half-sister (Octavia) was not part of Cleopatra's plan. The political union went ahead, the compromise being that Mark Antony could become her husband under Egyptian law, though not her king, the title kept for Caesar's son, her eldest, Caesarion. Mark Antony later renounced his marriage to Octavia, insulting Rome.

Octavian, Caesar's legal heir, and now Mark Antony's arch enemy, defeated him and his forces on land and sea, prompting his suicide. A devastated Cleopatra was put under house arrest by Octavian who was not influenced by Cleopatra's wiles. Her theatrical suicide, the result of the bite from an asp hidden, supposedly, under figs brought in by her servant, is substantiated by various sources; but they also collectively agree that such a bite, alone, would not have produced the pain-free death attributed to her, that poison was the main cause of death.

Her death is not the only mystery, of course. Whether she had her king-brother-husband killed in the way she had her sister killed … plenty of historians and writers have tried, and failed, to find a definitive answer.

DIGBY, Jane 1807–81

The daughter of an Admiral and a Viscountess, educated, and beautiful too, Jane mixed in the right circles and was swept off her feet when just seventeen by a Baron twice her age. Three years after their marriage, his taking a mistress may have prompted Jane to start her own string of affairs, starting with a lowly librarian from near her family's home in Holkham, Norfolk and progressing to her cousin Colonel Anson, who was probably the father of her son, Arthur (1828–1830).

Lady Jane Digby.

When he tired of her, she switched her attentions to the besotted Prince Felix Schwarzenberg, the Austrian attaché, who was living in Harley Street. The affair was not handled discreetly, and, again, Jane became pregnant but this time the relationship was stronger and she followed the Prince to Switzerland, where he had been sent when the affair surfaced. Her husband finally started divorce proceedings, the case causing a media sensation at a time when divorce was so rare that it needed an Act of Parliament before it went ahead; and a time when most women were happy to be stay-at-home wives, keeping any affairs behind firmly closed doors. She received a generous settlement and gave birth to the Prince's daughter in Basle, only to find that his Catholicism and career plans prevented him from marrying her.

It was Jane who was now besotted and she followed Felix to Germany, where King Ludwig of Bavaria noticed her and may have become her next lover. In the meantime, the German Baron Karl von Venningen pursued her and even assumed paternity of her next child in 1833, whether his or not. She agreed to marry Karl in spite of the feelings she still had for Felix and her lack of feeling for Karl, becoming a mother again, but this time accepted at court and high society. That was until she fell for a hell-raising Greek count, Spiridion Theotoky, (the antithesis of her husband) who apparently fought Karl in a duel, this seemingly the trigger that finally ended her marriage.

Jane converted to Greek orthodox and married her count five years later, giving birth to a son. The marriage in 1841 was again damaged by her husband's infidelity, leading promptly to her own adultery with none other than King Otto of Greece, but the couple stayed together until their son died, aged six, falling from a balcony. This drove Jane away and she now devoted herself, for a while, to travel, becoming the mistress of an Albanian general living in the mountains with a brigand army; until he slept with her French maid. This was the infidelity that seemed to push her towards renouncing men, but in fact it was to be the next man who became the love of her life.

This was Sheikh Medjuel, a Bedouin nobleman twenty years her junior, who she met when he was her guide across the Syrian desert, having toyed, admittedly, with one or two other local Arabs *en route*. They married in 1854 and this time there were no children – she had not maintained regular contact with the two that had survived childhood. Jane learned Arabic to add to her repertoire of languages (she already spoke eight) and adopted the local dress. She did not convert to Islam, though, but did dye her hair as blonde hair was considered unlucky by her husband. Her far-reaching search for love was over, and the couple spent six months of every year in a Damascus mansion and six months in nomadic tents in the desert. This anti-establishment and adventurous woman died as a result of a dysentery attack, aged seventy-four, leaving the Sheikh grief-stricken.

FISHER, Kitty, born FISCHER, Catherine c.1741–67

Born in London (probably Paddington) into a working class family of German emigrants, Kitty's beauty elevated her to the public eye by the age of seventeen. As a result, she caught the attention of some prominent figures of the day including the Prince of Wales and his brother, and – importantly – the portrait painter Sir Joshua Reynolds.

By the time she had her portrait painted (four times in all) by Sir Joshua between 1759 and 1766, she had already acquired a reputation as one of the top London courtesans. The paintings were

Kitty Fisher.

reproduced as cheap prints for her fans to buy, some small enough to sit secretly inside a snuff box or pocket watch. From working in a milliner's, she could soon afford to live in Mayfair.

Kitty's habit of riding at some speed in St. James's Park was frowned upon by some, and, following a fall which revealed her legs (a real shocker) and 'disordered' attire, a satirical print appeared in print around 1760 entitled 'The merry accident'… Some think this could have been a publicity stunt, in line with another stunt when she sandwiched a £20 banknote between two slices of bread and actually ate it to show her disdain for such a paltry sum of money! Some sources refer to £50 or even £100, a note first issued in 1725, but as even £20 is now worth thousands, this seems unlikely.

Apart from her appearance, and her equestrian skills, or otherwise, her extravagance was legendary, its funding earned in time-honoured fashion. Kitty was said to charge as much as one hundred guineas for one night, and enjoyed spending thousands on diamonds and magnificent clothing as well as out of season strawberries. She was well known at the gentlemen's clubs then in the West End (White's for example), and her liaisons were all with those of high status: politicians, barons, earls, merchants, army officers. Even Casanova – yes, that one – was an admirer.

None of her conquests offered her marriage however until John Norris, the MP for Rye came into her life, marrying her in 1766. He was not exactly a catch with his lack of moral restraint and his questionable finances, but Kitty settled into married life in the village of Benenden, Kent, amazing the locals with her prowess on horseback and earning a reputation for philanthropy.

Although the marriage lasted just a matter of months, this was because Kitty died suddenly in March 1767. A variety of reasons have been discussed over the years – consumption, lead poisoning from using cosmetics, smallpox … Whatever the reason, this short life was a full and famous one and she was apparently buried in one of her extravagant gowns. The courtesans at the time were the supermodels and celebrities of their day. Her name lives on in the expression 'My eye, Kitty Fisher' and the nursery rhyme about Lucy Locket: 'Lucy Locket lost her pocket, Kitty Fisher found it …'

HAMILTON, Emma 1765–1815

Although there are books galore devoted to the woman remembered as Nelson's mistress, this relationship filled just six years of her life. Her widowed mother brought her from the village of Ness, near Liverpool, to London and found her employment as a maid; by the age of sixteen she was 'working for' a Mrs Kelly, who had a brothel in the West End. Exceptionally beautiful, she caught the eye of a young baronet, Sir Harry Featherstonehaugh, who set her up as his mistress. Promiscuous by nature, she was said to have danced naked for him

Emma Hamilton.

and his friends – on the dining table. She is also said to have given birth to his daughter, brought up by her grandmother, but evidence for this is thin on the ground.

Tiring of her, Sir Harry handed her on to the Hon. Charles Greville, who financed her in return for her fidelity and who commissioned George Romney to paint her portrait. His finances were over-stretched however, so he abandoned her when a wealthy heiress came along and passed her on, in turn, to his uncle Sir William Hamilton. Sir William, the British minister in Naples, provided Emma with a social and musical education, both sadly lacking, and introduced her to theatre and culture. Five years later, in 1791, he married her on a visit to London – he was sixty and she was twenty-six.

Emma did not meet Nelson, other than briefly, until she was thirty-three, just as lovely but much heavier. He was married, fresh from his victory at the battle of the Nile (1798). She had laid on a huge party for him, with the streets of Naples decorated with the words 'Viva Nelson' at every turn. She also organised a great ball in his honour, using her contacts in the Italian royal family; Nelson was not just flattered, but besotted by her sexuality, her voluptuousness and her beauty. He also rather liked what had become her 'motherly' and nurturing nature, shown particularly during a dramatic escape by sea from Naples to Sicily (December 1798) when Nelson 'rescued' the Italian royal family, and the Hamiltons, from the danger of a French invasion – but on a stormy night, with Emma nursing the royal children. What others described as her coarse or vulgar nature did not deter him.

In 1800, the Hamiltons, accompanied by Nelson, had travelled back to England, and set up home as a *ménage a trois* in Piccadilly. It was not this threesome but more the fact that Nelson had left his wife that caused a public scandal; this just did not happen in high profile circles at the time.

Nelson's daughter, Horatia, was born in 1801, one of twins, though what happened to the second baby is a mystery. She may have died at birth, she may have been sent to a foundling hospital, or even to her grandmother. The couple settled in a house near Wimbledon, but William was still part of the family and they were at his side when he died in 1803. Nelson and Emma did manage to spend time together with their daughter, but he was spending more time at sea, commanding the British fleet in the Mediterranean and still fending off the French. A baby girl born during this period did not survive more than a few days (although, again, there are stories …)

His death at the battle of Trafalgar in 1805 sent Emma into shock, but did not dampen her hedonistic lifestyle which included a penchant for gambling and drinking. She now owned her home, courtesy of Nelson, and had an inheritance from Sir William, but still ran up huge debts and spent time in the debtors' prison in Southwark in 1813. To escape her creditors, she went to Calais soon after her release, with her daughter, but she died there in 1815, unrecognised.

KEPPEL, Alice (1868–1947)

Although Alice, as the daughter of Sir William Edmonstone, spent her formative years in Duntreath Castle on Loch Lomond, it is likely that she was actually born in Woolwich where her father was the supervisor of Woolwich Dockyard prior to his succeeding to the baronetcy in his later years. She was educated at home which she shared with eight siblings, all but one female and all older.

A striking looking young woman, she fell for George Keppel, an officer in the Gordon Highlanders. Although the son of an Earl, there was no cash to spare for the big city lifestyle they enjoyed and it seems they came to an agreement that she would take moneyed lovers to support them both. As a courtesan, she started with barons (Ernest Beckett followed by Humphrey Sturt), working her way up the aristocratic ladder until, aged twenty-nine, she met the fifty-six-year-old Prince of Wales, promptly becoming his newest mistress (there had been numerous women before her). The relationship did not falter when he became King Edward VII in 1901 – in fact, she became a leading and respected personality at court, bringing up the two daughters of her marriage (the eldest, Violet, not necessarily her husband's) in the royal entourage.

Alice Keppel.

Alice became the King's last and longest-serving mistress; it seems she was able to defuse his moods and keep him amused, becoming *la favorita* as a result, accompanying him on trips overseas. Another feather in Alice's cap was her political judgment and gift of intelligent conversation. The King's generosity allowed the Keppels to enjoy a London home in Grosvenor Street.

Queen Alexandra was as aware of Alice as she had been of her predecessors, but was less forgiving in private for, on his deathbed in 1910, when Alice wanted to be with him, the queen asked her to leave, causing quite a scene. Her influence immediately disappeared and it seems she was not even allowed to sign the book of condolence. The Keppels sold their home after the First World War, progressing to a villa in Florence where Alice revelled in Florentine society, although they returned home during the Second World War, staying in the Ritz Hotel. After fifty-six years of marriage, Alice died in Florence in September 1947, of liver disease, and is buried there – her husband died two months later.

Postscript: Alice has some interesting descendants – her eldest daughter, Violet Trefusis, was a lover of Vita Sackville-West and her great-grand-daughter is Camilla Parker Bowles.

LANGTRY, Lillie 1853–1929

Famous as the mistress of the Prince of Wales (later Edward VII), this red-haired daughter of the Dean of Jersey caused many other scandals during her lifetime. In fact, the affair with the Prince – or 'Bertie' – lasted only around three years following their meeting at a society dinner in 1877, initiated by Bertie it seems, such was Lillie's early fame as a beauty.

A couple of years earlier, she had married Irish landowner Edward Langtry, who had been visiting Jersey on his yacht, although this had not been her first proposal, given her vivacious personality and good looks. They set up home in London and although a

Lillie Langtry.

disappointing husband, less wealthy than he at first appeared as well as being a fop and reputed drunkard, he opened the doors to London society for Lillie. Bertie was charmed and made Lillie his official mistress, his wife and her husband turning a blind eye as was the protocol of the time.

During this period, any invitations sent to the Prince had to include Mrs Langtry and she was presented in court to Queen Victoria in 1878, the same year she was provided with a substantial 'love-nest' in Bournemouth by her royal lover. Other lovers included the wealthy Sir Robert Peel, Crown Prince Rudolf of Austria, and Prince Louis of Battenberg (the Duke of Edinburgh's grand-father) who is the reputed father of her only child, a daughter born in 1881.

Her fame resulted in her being offered work as an artist's model and as the face of Pears soap, and her image (as Jersey Lily) was reproduced on postcards. After her husband became bankrupt, she became the first society woman to appear on stage, following her ambition to be an actress – making her debut in *She Stoops to Conquer* at the Haymarket Theatre in 1881. She went on to play in Shakespeare, and toured America from 1885 to 1890, where the infamous Judge Roy Bean became a fan and named his saloon in Texas after her.

Lillie divorced her husband in 1887 and became an American citizen and a successful vineyard owner (there is still a Langtry Estate and Vineyard in California) thanks to all the cash she had accumulated from admirers, not to mention the jewellery and property and even racehorses. She returned to the London stage in 1892 (aged thirty-eight) basing herself in London's West End. But she found it even more profitable to turn her talents to the macho world of horse-racing, as an owner and as a gambler, both of which kept her in touch with her old 'friend' the Prince of Wales. She married the younger (by eighteen years) racehorse owner Hugo de Bathe in 1899, and now had enough money to purchase her own theatre, the Imperial in London.

While the scandals had dissipated, Lillie did not stagnate in retirement – she tried vaudeville in 1907, broke the bank at Monte Carlo (where she was living) in 1909, wrote a novel in 1910 and appeared in a film – *His Neighbour's Wife* – in 1916. Until her death in Monaco in 1929, she continued to act to benefit various charities and published her autobiography. Her grave is in the church in Jersey where her father became Dean – St. Saviour's – coming full circle.

LETESSIER, Caroline c.1830–84

The least known of the French courtesans in this book is included because of this but also because of her rags to riches back to rags story. There are records of a foster-father in her younger years so she may have been illegitimate, or orphaned. The only evidenced dates attached to her are her years as a young actress (1855–1858) at the Theatre du Palais Royal in Paris but there are also undated references to her appearances before this at the French Theatre in Turin. Certainly it seems that her elegance and wit had established her attraction for diplomats and members of the aristocracy in Italy before she moved on to Paris.

Certainly she did not come from a moneyed background but, in her twenties, featured at every important event in Paris, where she was renowned for her luxurious accessories including a golden apple for her powder and a lorgnette studded with precious stones. Actresses did not command that level of earning power, so there was no doubt that Caroline earned her money elsewhere, and was possibly more prostitute than courtesan. But not your everyday prostitute …

In 1859, she went to St Petersburg, where she lived comfortably for eight years. She borrowed the title of Princess Dolgorouki without her permission, and attracted more than one member of the royal family, including an anonymous 'Grand Duke' who came to her rescue at a ball where her dress was torn while waltzing. Unfortunately, it seems he used his diamond-encrusted cross of St. Andrew (awarded for outstanding service to the State) for this repair, which did not go down at all well and the Grand Duke himself risked exile to Siberia by abusing the award in this way. Some reports merely say that she wore the cross in a stage box, without reference to the torn dress.

The couple felt it necessary to move away from Russia and travelled to Germany, with one hiccup en route when the Berlin chief of police identified the Grand Duke as a nephew of Emperor Alexander and advised him to return; but he found a way around this and life continued in a luxury villa in Baden. Their favourite haunt seems to have been the local casino, with Caroline suitably dressed to impress.

Caroline did not stay in Baden, however, but whether she and her lover parted company or whether this was her own decision is lost in history. She seems to have been in Paris at some point during the Siege of 1870–71 and also turns up in Oxford soon after, staying at the Randolph Hotel with her friend Caroline Hasse. In Oxford, she captivated at least one young don, and, more famously, Ralph Waldo Emerson, the American poet.

Where she met the Prince of Monaco's son (presumably Prince Albert I) is not known but it seems she became his mistress, the last of her famous conquests. She ended her days as the proprietor of a hotel in Paris, helped by handouts from friends, having spent all the fortune she had acquired from her days as a courtesan – or prostitute.

MONTEZ, Lola c.1821–61

Born Elizabeth Gilbert in Ireland, her father's army posting to India in 1823 (he died soon after) resulted in her spending her childhood with an array of influences. She lived with relatives in Scotland from 1826 and went to boarding school in Bath from 1832, returning to India five years later. At this stage, her mother wanted to marry her off to a rich sixty-year-old but Eliza avoided the plan by eloping with an army officer nearer to her own age and they married in Ireland.

Lola Montez.

After a couple of years back in India, Eliza returned alone to live with relatives in England, but her adulterous affair during (and after) the voyage home led to her husband suing her for divorce, which went through in 1842. Resolving to go on to the stage, she travelled to Cadiz to learn Spanish dancing, re-inventing herself as Lola Montez. Her unique dance, which involved miming the death of a spider, brought her fame back in England (from 1843) although her claim to be Spanish caused her some problems. So she tried Germany, where she had mixed reviews, as she did in Poland, her temper leading her into trouble, in that she assaulted representatives of the law in both locations; she caused such uproar in Poland that she was deported. Such demonstrations sealed her notoriety.

Deciding that her next conquest would be high profile, she had a brief fling with the composer Liszt and then apparently with the writer Alexandre Dumas and the publisher Alexandre Dujarier. After applying to appear at the Theatre Royal in Munich in 1846, she met the King of Bavaria, Ludwig I, and he was smitten. Even though his cabinet resigned in protest, he made her a countess in 1847, meaning that Lola was now in danger of assassination. She fled the country when a mob stormed her villa and re-surfaced in London where she married again but the relationship was stormy, ending in 1851 when she could be seen on stage in New York, shocking people with her habit of smoking in public.

This was the time of the gold rush, and Lola, having married yet again (a newspaper editor, and an even shorter liaison) found that her spider dance went down well in California, and in 1855 had similar success in the gold-mining towns of Australia. Her manager there became her lover, but he was lost overboard when they were on their way back to San Francisco and an Austrian baron took his place briefly in Lola's bed. Although still popular in the U.S.A. and Canada, Lola, reputedly ill with syphilis, renounced stage work in 1857 to become a successful lecturer, with a particular interest in spiritualism and the power of the feminine, which funded her purchase of a large house in Park Lane, London. Planned as a fashionable boarding house, business was not her forte and her financial problems took her back to New York to more well paid lectures, until a stroke in 1860, followed by pneumonia, put an end to her spirited adventures and her travels. The *New York Times* wrote of her 'wonderfully chequered' career, although that is putting it mildly…

The inimitable Lola Montez – courtesan, dancer, actress, traveller, mistress, lecturer, – may have started life in a sleepy village in County Sligo but she was buried in New York; as Eliza Gilbert.

MURRAY, Fanny (Frances) 1729–78

Fanny is a prime example of a popular eighteenth century courtesan, being the equivalent of twenty-first century super-models, albeit with more voluptuous physiques. Sources are undecided as to whether she was born in Bath or London, but agree that her father was an impoverished musician and that she had become a flower-seller by the age of twelve.

Before becoming a teenager, her symmetrical beauty was already attracting attention, and she was seduced by the Duke of Marlborough's grandson (Jack Spencer), who quickly tired of such a young conquest. Beau Nash was next, but the age difference – he was in his sixties – meant that Fanny soon grew bored and tried for independence, becoming a London prostitute. This saw Fanny at her lowest ebb, needing to pawn her clothes to pay for treatment for the pox. She succumbed, out of desperation, to a procuress who also served as her landlady. It seems she managed to 'save' a few guineas so that she could escape and move on to a better class of lover, attracting a range of aristocrats and politicians. One of these, Lord Sandwich, was said to have introduced her to the antics of the notorious Hellfire Club, and she apparently attended parties there, dressed as a blasphemous nun.

Such progress meant that she was included in the 1747 *List of Covent Garden Ladies*, which meant she could increase her fee to at least two guineas a time and no doubt much more. Fanny had to pay the publisher for the privilege, however, and submit to an examination to show she was clear of venereal disease, but, for her, it was well worth it. She attracted leading portrait painters, became a muse for the literati and was set up in a Clapham house by Sir Richard Atkins, perhaps the most generous of her influential clients. She became the toast of the town, her glamour popular with the public, although servants described her as petulant and impetuous.

However, when Sir Richard died in 1756, Fanny was arrested for debt, and turned to the son of her first seducer, fifteen years earlier, who indeed came to her rescue. She continued for a short time as an active member of the London Whores' Club (which had about 100 members), until she married the actor David Ross in around 1757 and seems to have become a respectable housewife in Scotland. One source suggests that John Spencer paid David Ross an allowance to maintain her, to make amends for what his father did. A nice full-circle touch.

NEWBOROUGH, Lady Denisa 1913–87

Perhaps the last of the courtesans, Denisa (born Denisa Braun) left her Serbian home in her teens and – if her autobiography is to be believed – joined the circus as a wire-walker but tried a variety of other jobs before the Second World War. These included working as a fan dancer, a stripper, a nightclub hostess and even a pilot! At the outbreak of war, she became a transport officer with the British Red Cross until after her marriage to the 6th Baron Newborough, twice her age, in 1942. One of her 'qualifications' for her Red Cross work was her multi-lingual ability, but in spite of this she was dismissed when it was established that she was not British-born.

It wasn't just the aristocratic Tommy (i.e. the Baron) that danced attendance on the lovely flame-haired Denisa. It seems her admirers included a whole range of famous names from Hitler to the King of Spain and an un-named sheikh who presented her with 500 sheep. At one point, she was the mistress of five men simultaneously, all of whom seem to have presented her with a house or apartment.

In spite of this, her gambling habit (at bridge) led her to bankruptcy a few years after she and Tommy divorced. By now, she was famous only for being famous, like many current day 'celebrities'. But her 'name' meant she was able to re-invent herself as, rather unexpectedly given her prior occupations, a hat designer. Her most famous design was a hat covered in half smoked cigarettes, so she was certainly an original. She claimed her inspiration for her designs was French haute couture, and her accent suggested an authentic background for such claims. Other designs were 'Pirate', 'Milady' and 'Chic' with velvet a favoured fabric. In 1953, to counteract the smogs, she even designed a classy mask with gold sequins. All of these designs were featured in national newspapers during the early 1950s and worn by such luminaries as 1950s' film stars. You can see some of her designs on the British Pathe Films website. So successful was she, she was able to pay back many of her debts.

In 1958, Denisa wrote that there was no such thing as a vulgar piece of jewellery, whatever its size. She also announced that there were two occupations she would never consider – being a spy, or a whore. Hmm. This was particularly interesting given that in 1964 she was convicted of using her Mayfair home for 'habitual prostitution'; she was fined £50 plus £38 costs. Despite a successful appeal, this is when Lady Newborough disappears from the limelight.

PEARL, Cora 1835–86

Born less glamorously as Eliza Emma Crouch in Devon, her family struggled financially, especially when her music-teacher father emigrated to America without them. Eliza was sent to convent school in France, returning at nineteen to her grandmother's London home.

In her memoirs, Eliza recounts a Sunday when she was followed from church by a middle-aged man (apparently a diamond merchant), who invited the well-built redhead to a drinking den. He left her 'unconscious' in his bed with, allegedly, a £5 note. This enabled her to pay for a Covent Garden room.

Recognising a new power over men, she promptly became the mistress of the proprietor of the Argyll Rooms 'evening club' – for the wealthy – in Great Windmill Street. When they travelled to France as husband and wife, Eliza decided she preferred life there, adopted the name Cora Pearl and stayed on, alone.

Living humbly in Paris she attracted numerous lovers, the first high-profile figure being Victor Massena (the grandson of one of Napoleon's generals) who supplied expensive dresses and jewellery. He also funded her servants, including a chef, and her gambling habit. Cora was

Cora Pearl.

now able, to Victor's chagrin, to attract further lovers including the much younger Prince Achille Murat, who gave her a horse. With a new passion for equestrianism, Cora found a house with stables and added more than sixty fine horses, employing English grooms.

Parisian women copied her pale blue carriage, her clothes, and even her suntan (previously unfashionable), while Cora seduced their husbands and lovers. She added the Prince of Orange to her list of conquests along with the Emperor's half-brother, the Duc de Morny.

Cora treated herself to a chateau, near Orleans, with Wilton carpets, parquet floors and black silk sheets, spending a fortune on entertaining. Famously, at one of her dinners, she served herself up naked on a large silver salver, sprinkled with parsley. Such behaviour did not deter Prince Napoleon, who became her lover in 1868, three years after the Duc de Morny died. This became possibly her longest relationship, lasting some nine years, during which time she had a key to the Palais Royal and a monthly allowance of 12,000 francs.

Cora was now the toast of the town, incredibly rich, retaining her English accent and still sporting revealing gowns and such embellishments as diamond encrusted boots. An appearance on stage as Cupid attracted scathing criticism but Cora was oblivious. Admirers such as the Russian

Prince Paul Demidoff sent such gifts as candied chestnuts wrapped in a thousand-franc note, a silver horse and a roomful of orchids. She carried on gambling away thousands, paying an enormous staff, ordering toiletries from London, and introducing modern make-up and hair dye to her peers. Meanwhile, she was also attracting attention by her behaviour, for instance, a duel with another courtesan over a European prince, using riding-whips.

After the Siege of Paris (when she apparently showed a different side to her character; turning her main home into a small hospital) she arranged to meet Prince Napoleon at the Grosvenor Hotel in London, but the manager turned her away when he recognised her, leaving them to make alternative arrangements.

Around 1872, another younger lover, millionaire Alexandre Duval, gave her a hundred-page book, each page a thousand-franc note, but he couldn't keep up with her demands financially and she dismissed him. He returned with a revolver (his intent unclear) and wounded himself badly. The scandal resulted in her banishment – briefly – from France, so she moved around and gradually sold off her French assets, losing Napoleon's financial backing in 1874 when he decided to concentrate on 'a life of work'.

Reduced to charging a few francs for her favours to stave off total poverty, Cora died of cancer, aged fifty-one. Her fortune was gone but she had certainly enjoyed spending it.

SHORE, Jane c.1445–c.1528

Londoner Jane (christened Elizabeth) had parents who could afford to ensure she had a good education with some emphasis on playing musical instruments and speaking the Norman French of the day. These abilities, and her good looks, attracted many local young apprentices and she became known as the Rose of London. The word spread so that members of the court came to her father's shop ostensibly to buy silks and laces but in fact to admire the young woman sewing in the corner.

Lord Hastings, the Lord Chamberlain, is the first documented devotee, but Jane was oblivious to his attempts at seduction and apparently managed to avoid his plan to carry her off, thanks to her father's intervention. To avoid a repetition of this situation, her father found her a wealthy but unattractive husband, William Shore, twice her age (she was fifteen). Although Jane tried to hold out, Shore was persistent and she succumbed to his expensive gifts and loyalty.

The marriage was not a success. Jane was bored, childless, spending her time in her husband's jewellery shop or at home. The young court gallants – including Lord Hastings – renewed their attentions, becoming customers at the jeweller's. When William became suspicious and turned Hastings away from his shop, Hastings described her assets and charms

Jane Shore doing public penance.

to his royal master, Edward IV, resulting in an invitation for Jane (and her husband) to attend a masked ball. William Shore was not a party man but allowed Jane to attend, with a chaperone, and she was invited to dance by a mysterious masked man …

The King, unmasked, was a notorious womaniser, married and with at least one other mistress, but Jane had no hesitation in leaving her supposedly impotent husband. The marriage was finally annulled in 1476, well after her relationship with the King was established and she had been installed in a magnificent suite at the court. Jane seems to have become his favourite mistress and seemingly the one that lasted the longest – in spite of her being pursued, still, by Lord Hastings and by others such as the king's younger brother, Richard, Duke of Gloucester.

It was only Edward's death in 1483 that brought an end to the affair. Jane took up with the Marquis of Dorset, but this was the opportunity that Hastings had been waiting for and Jane finally succumbed. But this did not go down well with Richard who was now the Protector (in control of the twelve-year-old Edward V).

In the meantime, Richard had managed to persuade the courts that Edward's two young sons were illegitimate and they were imprisoned in the Tower of London allowing him to be proclaimed as King Richard III (the boys subsequently 'disappeared'). Now he was in a position to accuse the couple of treachery and of witchcraft, plotting against him and potentially responsible for his spinal deformity! Hastings was executed in 1483, following an inadequate trial, and Jane was imprisoned, firstly in the Tower and latterly in Ludgate Prison.

Was Richard III perhaps furious with Jane's earlier rejection – because he wasn't finished with her, accusing her of harlotry! She was found guilty and sentenced to public penance at St. Paul's where the public could throw mud and stones at her en route – although it seems that the crowd were too sympathetic to actually do this. The penance was followed by her being cast into the streets, penniless. Richard, again had her arrested but this time she was visited in prison by the King's Solicitor General, Thomas Lynom, who offered marriage – after all she was still in her early thirties and still beautiful.

Her final years, following her husband's death in 1518, are a mystery, as are specific details of her (two?) children from this last marriage. Sir Thomas More, who had recorded his meetings with Jane in his youth, wrote of her again in 1527 as poverty-stricken though this seems unlikely.

VILLIERS, Barbara c.1640–1709

The only child of aristocratic parents, by the time she was seventeen she was the mistress of the Earl of Chesterfield, continuing the affair after marrying Roger Palmer when she was nineteen. In the meantime, she had met Charles II (how and where is unknown) and he acknowledged the daughter she bore in February 1661 (not his first illegitimate child). He had been in London since May 1660 following the restoration of

Barbara Villiers.

the monarchy, which had enabled him to return from exile.

When pregnant by Charles, Barbara became a countess when Palmer was made Earl of Castlemaine. Her son was born around the time Charles married the Portuguese Catherine of Braganza in the summer of 1662.

Baptised as Catholic by Palmer, this son was re-christened in the Church of England per the King's instructions, dividing the Palmers irrevocably. Barbara then became one of the ladies of the queen's royal bedchamber, over-riding objectors. The Countess of Castlemaine certainly attracted attention with her blue eyes and near-black hair. She was painted by Peter Lely, the court painter, and took a leading role at court events. Charles was not her only admirer; the courtier Henry Jermyn has been named as another long-term lover, perhaps causing Charles to delay acknowledging the son she bore in September 1663. Nevertheless, she dined with the King frequently and she was hostess at a dinner for the French ambassador.

With two more children in 1664 and 1665, she was winning more advantage over the childless queen and was living in style at lavish apartments in Whitehall, visited often by Charles. Barbara did have competition, however, in the form of Frances Stuart, a maid of honour, and the actress Mary Davis, her affair with Charles beginning in January 1668. Barbara was just as unfaithful, with an interesting variety of partners: a rope dancer; an actor; a playwright; and a duke! Nevertheless, she was seen early in 1668 wearing some of the crown jewels at court, and Charles purchased a house opposite St James's Palace for her in May.

Her power over the King produced enemies, naturally, but the King resented any hostility shown towards Barbara and always took her side. He seems to have turned a blind eye to her extravagance, even to her plundering the privy purse.

It was the arrival of other royal mistresses (including Nell Gwynn) that diminished Barbara's powers. The child she bore in 1672 was never acknowledged by Charles. The King had done her proud financially, with titles, pensions, and property, with the acknowledged offspring being granted royal arms. Barbara was popular with the public, appearing with a coach and eight horses in the streets where she was cheered by passers-by, but her Catholicism forced her resignation from the queen's bedchamber in 1673.

Now Duchess of Cleveland, another title, Barbara moved to France with her daughters in 1676, which appears to have been done to economise. Her lovers in France seemed to have included the English ambassador and the Marquis de Chatillon – her love letters to the latter apparently intercepted and forwarded on to Charles. He postponed seeing Barbara on her return to England in 1682, which may have been why she started an affair with actor Cardell Goodman two years later. Cardell was reputedly a highwayman(!) who was jailed for attempting to poison her sons and was eventually exposed as a Jacobite conspirator which sent him into exile.

At sixty-four, Barbara made another poor choice. She married gold-digger Beau Fielding in 1705 who was not only already married, but who began an affair with her grand-daughter. When confronted with the bigamy charge, Fielding attacked Barbara, and was arrested and had his hand burned as punishment. The marriage was annulled in 1707 after she had sued Fielding for adultery but her adventures were now over. She died of dropsy two years later, one of the first acknowledged royal mistresses for many years, and regarded as the most influential.

WILSON, Harriette (born Dubouchet, Harriette) 1786–1845

An interesting combination of courtesan (a whore with classy clients!) and blackmailer, Harriette was one of the fifteen children of a Swiss clock-maker and a stocking mender from Marylebone in central London. She took herself off to Brighton at fifteen, having decided that her eldest sister had the sort of lifestyle that appealed to her (Amy was known to be the mistress of the Duke of Argyll, among others), although aware that she was not beautiful. A third sister, Sophy, followed a similar career path and the three girls were known at one point as The Three Graces.

Harriette's personality and exuberance soon secured the thirty-one--year old Earl of Craven as her first conquest. It seems he was a bit of a disappointment, however, and she was bored by his stories of his cocoa trees in the West Indies and his practice of wearing a nightcap.

Lord Craven was the first of a sequence of lovers, with those succeeding him over the next couple of decades all possessing titles, the Prince Regent among them. Her liaisons enabled her to live in grand houses, wear expensive clothes, and throw expensive parties. She also seems to have benefited from a pay-out by the Duke of Beaufort, a bribe to ensure she did not marry his heir.

As the natural home of the nineteenth century courtesan, Paris was her destination in 1820, from where she continued her liaisons with the British nobility. Realising that these men would pay to avoid scandal, she began writing her memoirs, but granted those who paid £200 immunity from appearing within the pages! Whether the Duke of Wellington did indeed tell her to 'publish and be damned' is unconfirmed but seems entirely likely – and his inclusion certainly helped sales of the book.

The book, published in 1825, ran to thirty editions in the first year alone in spite of its literary limitations – those famous names were the attraction. Harriette and her publisher had to literally fight off those looking for copies, and they made as much as £10,000 – plus all those payments of £200 that went unrecorded. She threatened further publications, securing her more hush money over the next few years, also attempting a couple of novels.

With the earning power of a courtesan/mistress always limited by time, Harriette was financially able to 'retire' and eventually married the man she had rescued from debtors' prison in 1826 – 'Colonel' William Rochfort, an ex-soldier with a shady reputation. Now ostracised as a result of her memoirs and having been accused of assaulting her maid, the couple moved back to France until his death when she returned to her English roots, ending her days in Chelsea in 1845.

Chapter Two

Madams, Prostitutes and Adulterers

BOLEYN, ANNE c.1502–36 & MARY BOLEYN c.1499–1543

The two sisters, daughters of Sir Thomas Boleyn, a minor courtier, were despatched to France to the court of Louis and Henry VIII's sister Mary in 1514, Anne aged just twelve or possibly even younger as there is historical dispute with regard to her date of birth. Anne was seemingly more intelligent, but less attractive, than Mary, being very dark eyed with skin that bordered on sallow and unfashionably small-breasted. Whether she had an extra finger (regarded as a sign of witchcraft) is difficult to substantiate, although if she did indeed start a fashion for long sleeves covering the hands then that would seem a good enough reason.

Mary Boleyn.

Mary is reputed to have returned to England after acquiring a reputation from 1515 in the French court for being a 'great whore' according to Francis I, King of France, reputedly one of her conquests. She was married off to William Carey, a descendant of John of Gaunt, in 1520, and her three-year affair with Henry took place during this marriage, at which time she gave birth to a son and a daughter, either of whom

ANNA BVLLEN REGINA ANGLIÆ.
Henrici VIII' Vxor 2ª Elizabethæ Reginæ
Mater fuit decollata, Londini, 19 May Æ 1536.

Anne Boleyn.

could have been Henry's. William Carey was granted several gifts of land by Henry, a possible reward for overlooking his wife's adultery.

Following Mary back to England by 1521, Anne was appointed maid of honour to Queen Catherine. No sooner had Henry started to lose interest in Mary than his attention was caught by her younger sister. She had the personality, wit, and courtly accomplishments to attract the King, amongst others. Anne, according to some historians, refused the King's advances, making her all the more attractive in his eyes, a man not used to rejection. It seems unlikely that Anne's refusal was out of virtue, even though many have defended her from subsequent accusations of manoeuvring her way to the throne. If it had not been for Anne's stubborn refusal to become the King's mistress, the whole course of English history – and of Christendom – could have been very different. As it was, the only way for Henry to get into Anne's bed was by marrying her, breaking with Rome and divorcing Catherine. They did jump the gun, however, because it seems Anne was pregnant at the time of their secret marriage in 1533, before Henry's marriage had been annulled.

Unfortunately for Anne, of course, she failed to produce the male heir Henry needed – and how galling it must have been that her sister Mary had produced a healthy boy. So that Henry could marry yet again, Anne was accused of treason, witchcraft, adultery, even incest (with her brother George), the guilty verdict resulting – not unexpectedly – in the death sentence. Whether she was guilty of all, or any, of these charges, is open to prolonged debate. Death by the axe was a terrifying prospect and a swordsman was called from France to the Tower of London to sever the reputedly narrow neck with a sword instead of the usual axe.

Mary managed a quieter, more respectable, end. When William Carey died in 1528 of a 'sweating sickness', Henry ordered Thomas Boleyn to take Mary under his roof and maintain her, with an annuity of £100. However, in 1534 she secretly married William Stafford, a commoner. She was no longer received at court – thanks to her sister – and settled for a life of obscurity at Rochford Hall in Essex.

The debate as to the morals of these two sisters goes on, and on, and …

BORGIA, Lucrezia 1480–1519

The illegitimate daughter of a Cardinal (later a Pope), Lucrezia was married three times for political reasons by the age of twenty-two. From a power-hungry and scheming family, her name has become synonymous with corruption and bloodshed.

Lucrezia Borgia.

Unusually for an Italian woman, she had golden hair and became renowned as a young woman for her beauty. She was as young as ten when she became a tool for her father's political ambitions. Having entered into a marriage contract with a Spanish nobleman, her father regarded marriage to an Italian lord more advantageous, but their marriage was eventually annulled in 1497 when he lost favour with the Borgias. Her father had decreed that the marriage had not been consummated, but Lucrezia gave birth, in secret, three months after the annulment. The baby has been posited as the child of an incestuous relationship between Lucrezia and her brother, or even as the child of her relationship with the Pope's messenger, conveniently (?) murdered in 1498, but only Lucrezia knew the truth.

Still just eighteen, Lucrezia was next married off to Alfonso of Aragon, the son of the King of Naples. To be fair, there did seem to be a real affection between the couple. But Lucrezia was widowed at twenty when he was strangled by her brother Cesare, who regarded him as an obstacle to an Italian alliance with France. It seems unlikely that Lucrezia had a hand in this murder, as she was in mourning for some time following his death. Another marriage, in 1502, to another Alfonso, the Duke of Ferrara, resulted in several adulterous relationships on both parts, her most famous affair being with her brother-in-law which ended when he contracted syphilis. But the marriage produced several children and lasted until her death in 1519. This seems to have been the period when she was at her happiest but whether this was due to husband, amours or children …

The story of Lucrezia poisoning her enemies with arsenic kept in a hollow ring, and added to their drinks at dinner, seem to have been introduced by her enemies – political enemies or rivals for the affections of the men in her life – and are not generally taken too seriously by historians. Her reputation has become tainted over the years because of her links with the unsavoury members of her family; her brother, Cesare, her father, and her mother who was the father's favoured mistress for some years, producing Cesare and at least one other brother, Giovanni.

In 1512, she began to take an interest in religion, possibly affected by the death of her first son. Her final years were spent out of the public eye and she died ten days after giving birth to a stillborn daughter in June 1519, aged just thirty-nine.

CLAP, Margaret c.1682–c.1726

This lady ran a Holborn (London) brothel with a difference. It was described at the time as a 'sodomitical house' where investigating constables in 1725 found as many as fifty men, some dressed as women, indulging in 'gross behaviour' – including 'kissing in a lewd manner'. Mother Clap, as she was known, denied condoning such practices, her main defence being the fact that she was a woman!

She was certainly not alone, though her 'coffee house' may have been the most notorious. At least twenty such brothels (known as molly houses) were operating in central London at a time when homosexuality was illegal, resulting in a fine or worse in that the act was considered a capital offence. Margaret Clap also took in lodgers, not necessarily only male prostitutes, and was generally very obliging for her gay customers, providing them with alibis and character references as and when necessary. She was even said to have earmarked one particular room as 'The Chapel' where clients could indulge in a mock marriage. It is perfectly possible that Mother Clap fulfilled her role as much for pleasure as for profit, making her money mainly from the sale of alcohol brought in from a nearby tavern.

The constables who had raided her (and other) premises arrived courtesy of an embittered homosexual called Partridge who had turned informant because he was so furious at being 'outed' by his gay lover. The premises had in any case been under surveillance by the Society for the Reformation of Manners, so plenty of evidence had been collected against Mother Clap.

In July 1726, Margaret Clap was sentenced to two years in prison, along with a fine of twenty marks. The sentence did not take effect, however, because when she was placed in the pillory at Smithfield – part of her punishment, prior to her serving her sentence – the public assaulted her so viciously that she fainted, and is believed to have died of her injuries soon after.

The trial proceedings can be seen on the Old Bailey website, which makes for a fascinating insight into the mind-set of the time. By August, three male prostitutes connected with Mother Clap were hanged at Tyburn but Partridge escaped prosecution.

Nothing is known of Margaret Clap's earlier life quite possibly because her name, both Margaret and Clap being slang terms, could be a fabrication. There are references to her husband, John Clap, in some sources, but, assuming he existed, he certainly does not figure largely and was never arrested or tried. However, there is a record of two daughters being born in St Dunstan's, Stepney, as the children of John and Margaret Clap – Elizabeth in 1705/06 and Martha in December 1707.

COLETTE, Sidonie (known by her surname) 1873–1954

Her most famous book, *Gigi* (made into a film), was not published until Colette was seventy-two, in 1944, but all those earlier years were put to good use. The fact that she was born in a commune in central France, with a radical Afro-Caribbean mother who was anti-marriage and pro-lesbianism, gives some idea of her start in life.

Colette at the Moulin Rouge.

Well-educated, she started writing as a teenager, erotic stories about a lusty teenager called Claudine, and married a publisher when she was twenty. Her husband was fifteen years older and saw the commercial potential for lewd publications – this was Henri Gautier-Villars, known as Willy. In spite of his many mistresses, the marriage lasted thirteen years, with Colette producing plenty of popular, titillating books for Willy. Whether he actually locked her up in a room to produce these novels has never been proven, but there seems to be no doubt that he encouraged her interest in lesbianism.

Colette's interest in sex led her to a different profession after their divorce – she became known as a music hall artiste, transferring eroticism to the stage with mime and dance. Her six-year relationship with the aristocratic, masculine Missy (Mathilde de Morny) had already begun before the end of her marriage. Scandal only erupted in 1907 when they appeared on stage together at the Moulin Rouge, Colette embracing Missy openly while naked. The two women were also known to visit Natalie Barney's lesbian night club in Paris, among other similar establishments that were notorious at the time.

Describing herself as sexually 'impartial' Colette's second marriage was to the father of the child she was expecting in 1912, a man as virile and as promiscuous as his wife. Their open, adulterous marriage lasted until she went too far – having an affair with her teenage stepson, Bertrand, which husband Henry regarded as incestuous. Her writing had continued apace during this period and in her lifetime she produced more than fifty novels, being heralded as France's leading woman writer.

Maurice Goudeket, her final husband, was made of sterner stuff. He accepted Colette's behaviour and remained devotedly loyal until her death, becoming known, apparently, as Mr Goodcock. A pearl salesman, Maurice was seventeen years younger than his wife. While married to him, she opened a beauty parlour in Paris (Colette's Institut de Beaute), at the age of sixty. He was taken into custody by the Gestapo (as a Jew) during the Second World War, with Colette's impassioned pleading to the German ambassador probably to thank for his release.

Her funeral, in 1954, was a state affair, unusual for a woman, as was the fact that she achieved the status of Grand Officer of the Legion d'Honneur the year before. She died an international celebrity who had led a fascinating, full – and versatile – life.

DEVINE, Matilda (known as Tilly) 1900–70

Born into a poor family in South London, Tilly left school age twelve to work in a sweatshop but dreamed of a glamorous life like that of the music hall performers and showgirls she admired. By the age of fifteen, she had concluded that prostitution offered more prospects, but could see that this was to be a temporary lifestyle, especially as she was arrested for soliciting soon after. A year later, she met Big Jim Devine, an Australian soldier, a former sheep-shearer and small time criminal who had actually gone AWOL, who offered her the escape she was looking for.

The couple married when Tilly was seventeen, with Big Jim returning to Australia two years later (after two children, one of whom died, the other left behind with her mother). He was followed by his bride and raised no objections to her continuing to do the kind of 'work' she was used to. Prostitutes were in demand in Sydney; demobbed troops were especially good customers (this was just after the First World War, of course).

Tilly was arrested over seventy times in the next five years, for whoring, fighting and offensive language or behaviour. Her violent husband drove the getaway car for the local villains, so that the couple acquired quite a reputation. In 1925, she opened her first brothel, with more than twenty more by the end of the 1930s, but her persona didn't change. She was still a violent fighter and had become a chain smoking heavy drinker, decked out in expensive jewellery and furs, regularly arrested for foul language and assault. In fact, she seems to have been arrested more times than anyone in Australia's history; some say over 200 arrests. Her longest sentence was two years, in the 1920s, for slashing a man with a cut-throat razor.

Her violence increased when another woman, Kate Leigh, came along to take on her crown – as only guns needed a licence, the Razor Gang Wars broke out between the two rivals. Kate made her money from liquor and cocaine but tried to muscle in on prostitution, resulting in years of violence, with prostitutes on both 'sides' being slashed and disfigured in violent battles. There was no truce until 1936 when the police commissioner stepped in, basically offering to leave them alone if they left each other alone!

After twenty-five years of abuse, Tilly finally divorced Jim in 1943, but re-married two years later, settling down, finally, with Eric Parsons, a merchant seaman, until he died in 1958.

She did return to Britain at one point during their marriage – to join the crowds outside Westminster Abbey who were cheering Queen Elizabeth at her coronation. But Australia's tax authorities finally got to her soon after her return, meaning that she had to sell her brothels and much of her jewellery.

Tilly was back to her poverty stricken roots, and died in obscurity, with just a handful of mourners at her funeral. However, she lingers on near the top of lists of Australia's 'worst' women or 'most famous female criminals' – she'd have liked that.

DUPLESSIS, Marie 1824–47

Born in Normandy to a violent father and a mother who left the family home to escape him, Alphonsine Plessis (her real name) was treated pretty much as a commodity from the age of fourteen. A renowned beauty, with shining black hair past her knees, her father initially sent her to work as a laundress, then making umbrellas, and then in a shop. It is quite possible he was also her pimp.

Before she was sixteen, she was finally given a home and a taste of the luxury she coveted in return for sexual favours by a series of ever more moneyed French lovers, including the Duc de Guiche Gramont. At the same time, she changed her name to Marie because of her admiration for the Virgin Mary and added the Du to Plessis to give it more 'class'.

After an affair with an anonymous vicomte (which apparently produced a baby who was quickly farmed out), the Baron de Stackelberg, old enough to be her father, took her on. He was apparently hoping to 'reform' her and gave her the luxury she craved, including a coach and horses and a Paris apartment lavishly decorated like a palace, which was full of flowers. But she soon grew tired of this celibate existence and returned to her old ways with lovers said to include Franz Liszt and the son of author Alexandre Dumas.

As the Queen of the Parisian demi-monde, Marie never missed a first night, and she gave a small fortune to charity. She became the epitome of respectability when she married French count, Edouard de Perregaux, in 1846, but she was already ill with consumption. He was already in debt. The marriage, not surprisingly, foundered and Marie tried to resurrect her hedonistic existence, but was prevented from doing so by her illness.

She died, stripped of her riches, aged just twenty-three. Some say a simple Breton peasant woman was there at the end, praying for her. Her mother perhaps? Eighteen months after her funeral, where her body had been shrouded in lace with a coffin full of flowers (including one of her favourites: camellias), and attended by her husband and the baron, Alexandre Dumas Junior published *La Dame aux camellias*. It has since become a play, an opera, spawned a number of films and a television series – continuing the legend that is Marie Duplessis, her youthful departure from life giving her added celebrity.

FERNSEED, Margaret (alt. spelling Fearnside) c.1560–1608

Margaret's background is one of those that would fit into more than one chapter for she was not just a prostitute, pimp, madam and blackmailer, but she was also a convicted killer. Starting at puberty as a prostitute she quickly progressed to brothel keeper, approaching young girls arriving in London for a new life but who ended up debauched and on the streets, paying Margaret for the privilege.

Married women were also persuaded into prostitution if they were unhappy with their husbands' level of (financial) support. Once they fell for the idea of a 'better' life they were trapped, because any refusal would mean that Margaret would contact their husbands.

Anthony, her own husband since 1593, was a London tailor, but it seems the pair did not live in the same house. Her brothel was near the Tower of London and he lived in Soho. Whether he knew about her activities is unknown, but surely very likely.

His body, with the throat cut, was found on Peckham Field in the autumn of 1607, seemingly dumped there, having been killed elsewhere. With a substantial amount of cash, and gold rings, upon the body, the motive was certainly not robbery. It was Margaret who identified his body – apparently with little emotion and no tears. Their unusual marriage and their rows – as reported by several witnesses – led to Margaret being the only suspect. She, perhaps not unexpectedly, denied all knowledge, confessing only to her other vice-related crimes. A pamphlet was published at the time, said to be authored by Margaret, detailing her role as a bawd and brothel keeper but with no suggestion that she had been involved in her husband's murder.

Following a spell in prison at the old county gaol based in the White Lion Inn in Southwark, she was tried and convicted on the hearsay of others. For example, a report of her having at one stage attempted to murder her victim with poisoned broth, also denied, was unproven. Two sailors who had lodged at her 'bad house' quoted her as describing her husband as a 'slave and villain' that she wanted 'rid' of. She was further accused of having a lover, who had fled, the evidence for this being that she was selling goods to fund their imagined reunion. There was reference to her 'slight regard' of Anthony in life – hardly a motive for murder.

Her execution was of its time; wearing a smock that was specially treated to facilitate burning, she faced an unpleasant death at the stake in St. George's Field in February 1608, but denied her guilt to the very end.

GARDNER, Ava 1922–90

A glamorous man-eater, unfazed by criticism of her private life, Ava was the ultimate bad girl of the silver screen, off and on. It was her sensual good looks and perfect figure that got her a screen test at eighteen, a virgin from a rural community in North Carolina, the youngest of seven children. The movies sounded like a ticket to fame and fortune, but she had not allowed for her lack of acting ability and her country accent.

Ava Gardner.

These shortcomings meant that she failed her first screen test, but nevertheless her stand-out looks got her a deal with MGM, where she met the biggest womaniser at the time in the unlikely form of Mickey Rooney. They married when she was just nineteen, but Mickey's womanising continued and the marriage lasted less than two years, leaving her with plenty of men to choose from including Howard Hughes (who she matched in violent drunken rages), actor Peter Lawford, band leader Artie Shaw (who she married: for twelve months) and George C. Scott, another actor.

Ava acquired a reputation for bedding her leading men whether married or not – Clark Gable, Robert Taylor, Kirk Douglas, Omar Sharif and Robert Mitchum among them. It seems there were few men in Hollywood who could out-drink Ava, someone who worked hard and played hard, but Frank Sinatra, her third husband, came close; reputably he was the love of her life. The marriage (1951–1957) was, predictably, stormy, with Ava having at least one abortion. A free spirit, she disregarded Frank's jealousy when she conducted an affair with a young bullfighter when filming in Spain.

This pretty much ended the marriage, but not Ava's interest in bullfighting and bullfighters, a world to which she had been introduced by Ernest Hemingway, a friend (but not a lover). She moved to Spain after divorcing Sinatra in 1957 and took up flamenco as well as learning the language, but her love of the country – and the matadors – did not last. She moved from the countryside to Madrid but could not settle, and moved to London in 1968 for a more sedate existence, having first to dry out at a health farm after years of partying.

A book of Ava's 'confessions', ghostwritten, was finally published in 2012, its earlier publication thwarted by Frank Sinatra who apparently paid her what she would have got from the book in 1988. She had felt it necessary to either publish the book or sell her jewellery, but had become 'fond' of the jewellery. It seems that Frank continued to help her financially, although she did appear as a guest in a number of episodes of *Knot's Landing* (an American soap opera) in 1985, having made over sixty films during her lusty career.

Ava ended her days in London, dying from emphysema in 1990, four years after a stroke, her heavy smoking a contributory factor to both. She is buried in the family plot in her home town – a small town, but a big name.

HOWARD, Frances 1593–1632

Daughter of Thomas Howard, Earl of Suffolk, Frances was married off to the Earl of Essex when she was thirteen and already admired for her beauty. This was a political move by the Howards, although the young couple were separated soon after because of their youth (he was fourteen) and the Earl sent off travelling to finish his education while she went back to her family. Upon his return, he was seemingly unable to consummate the marriage.

Unsurprisingly, Frances sought solace elsewhere, first with Prince Henry (d. 1612) and then with Robert Carr, who was to become the Earl of Somerset, a favourite of King James I, an even better political bet. There were accounts of Frances attempting to poison Essex at this stage, but any such attempt obviously failed and she petitioned for an annulment. This meant having a medical examination to establish her virginity – cleverly evaded, apparently, by substituting a young accomplice. She also had to deal with claims of witchcraft because apparently Essex was only impotent with her! The marriage was annulled in September 1613, leaving Frances free to marry Carr three months later.

Frances Howard.

However, it was not that simple. Days before the nullity, Thomas Overbury, who had opposed his good friend's marriage to the 'filthy, base' Frances, had died in the Tower where he had been imprisoned for refusing a mission from the king. In 1615, Gervase Elwes, the lieutenant of the Tower, revealed – when drunk – that Overbury had not died a natural death; he had been poisoned and finished off with a poisoned enema. Elwes had thwarted a plot by Overbury's keeper, Richard Weston, to murder Overbury and implicated Frances and her friend Anne Turner who had sent in wine, tarts and jellies with such additions as arsenic and mercury. The story matched that of William Reeve, an apothecary's assistant, confessing to his involvement on his deathbed.

This delighted the courtiers hostile to the Howards, who were also gleeful at finding 'evidence' that Frances had attempted to pay £1,000 to Sir David Wood to kill Overbury, a task he refused. Weston was tried, but it was Frances who was vilified as a syphilitic whore, a witch and a murdering sorceress, damaging Essex, seducing Carr and killing Overbury. The method used for the murder was regarded as alien to the English character, with the case becoming the biggest scandal of James I's reign.

It was probably Frances' confession that spared her life. After an unfair trial of all those involved, Robert Carr was also spared. It was Gervase Elwes, Richard Weston and Anne Turner who went to the gallows in November 1615, the first two for murder and the latter for complicity.

Frances and Robert remained in the Tower until 1622, with their daughter Anne who was born late in 1615, after they had been imprisoned. They lived out their lives in semi-isolation, and Frances died in Chiswick – of ovarian or uterine cancer – in 1632. She was buried at the family seat in Audley End, Essex.

JEFFRIES, Mary c.1820–c.1907

Although Mary was undoubtedly a prostitute herself as a young woman (from around 1840), she is better known as a madam. She saw what appears to have been a few gaps in the brothel market – for servicing the elite with the young and under-age (the age of consent was thirteen prior to 1885) and for providing sadomasochistic services.

Her brothels specialised effectively in perversions but were located in wealthy areas such as Chelsea and Kensington, with a flagellation house in Hampstead and a torture chamber in Gray's Inn. She was also suspected of trafficking girls overseas from a clearing house at Kew, conveniently on the river.

Because of the nature of her clients, Mary was protected from prosecution – by the police, the military and the establishment. A regular customer was said to be Sir William Harcourt, the Home Secretary, a nasty piece of work suspected of an incestuous relationship with his own son, and even King Leopold of the Belgians. The latter was said to have paid for young virgins aged between ten and fifteen to be shipped to Brussels for his 'entertainment'! The Prince of Wales – Edward VII to be – was also named.

Although a private prosecution was finally brought against her in 1885, the accusation did not go above 'keeping a disorderly house' for which she was fined £200 and told to 'find sureties [of £400] to be of good behaviour and keep the peace'. Referred to in newspapers as 'The White Slave Widow', it is interesting to note that she arrived at court in a carriage provided by a member of the House of Lords ...

It wasn't until 1887, after the law had changed, with the age of consent raised to sixteen, that Mary was finally put on trial. The period covered by the sureties had expired. This time she arrived in her own brougham, driven by a servant. Witnesses who lived in Brompton Square in particular spoke of the comings and goings at all hours and the indecorous behaviour, soliciting, and brawls taking place in the street. Although suspected of kidnapping some of the young girls in her service, no charges of kidnap were brought.

Mary had got away with her trade for several decades but finally she received a prison sentence, in spite of deteriorating health – although only for six months. But this seems to have been enough of a deterrent as she then disappeared from public view.

LAMB, Lady Caroline 1785–1828

Caroline was brought up in comfort and surrounded by culture, but was allowed to run wild unless restrained by her grandmother, Lady Spencer. Her lack of formal education and her access to travel meant that she grew into a teenage tomboy who enjoyed dressing as a boy and riding bareback.

However, on making her society debut in 1802 her spirited personality and skill at conversation captivated

Lady Caroline Lamb.

a number of status figures, including William Lamb, second son of Lord Melbourne. He was not regarded as a good catch until his older brother died, and they married a few months after this, in 1805. William was very protective of what can only be described as his volatile, intense wife, in spite of her emotional outbursts and risque outfits. He does not even seem to have been perturbed by a dinner party when his wife served herself up naked on a silver platter! Their only surviving child, Augustus, was born with learning difficulties in 1807, but the couple nevertheless seemed idyllic until their temperamental differences surfaced. He wanted peace and she wanted drama and romance.

Caroline's open infidelities provided the drama and romance she needed, but did not advance her husband's political career – he did not become Prime Minister until 1834. Her lifestyle also went down badly with her mother in law, Lady Melbourne, who was horrified by the flouting of public opinion

– for instance when Caroline openly accompanied the youthful Sir Godfrey Webster to society gatherings.

Her most famous affair was one of the shortest. When Lord Byron became famous overnight following the publication of *Childe Harold* in 1812, Caroline saw him as the romantic hero featured and not the sulky man with a lame leg who had introduced himself to her at Lady Holland's. Having heard that Caroline was not interested in him raised his expectations; he preferred women he had to pursue. Little did he know that she didn't need pursuing; she was attracted instantly to his 'beautiful pale face' and famously described him as 'bad, mad and dangerous to know'. They exchanged letters daily and she made him jealous by waltzing with other men, his club foot not allowing him to dance. But, having capitulated, and starting to talk about leaving her husband, she became less attractive to the contradictory Byron and he grew bored with her after less than nine months.

Their passionate affair had been the scandal of the year. But Caroline was not ready for it to end. She burnt his gifts to her when he terminated their affair, but was still fixated. Even a year later, when they were at the same ball, Caroline – whose behaviour was becoming more and more irrational – slashed her arms with a broken glass, taking a step too far where society was concerned.

Byron escaped by marrying in 1815 but the marriage foundered within a year and he left England for Europe, never to return. Caroline turned to writing novels, the first of which – *Glenarvon* – was based on her relationship with Byron, along with other stories of real people in fashionable society. Publication resulted in yet another scandal (although this also made the book successful of course).

In 1824, Caroline, who had produced another couple of novels in the meantime, became hysterical when she heard of Byron's death from a fever in Greece. She began to deteriorate with regard to her appearance, her moods and her behaviours. While during this period she became closer to her husband, she also became too fond of brandy and laudanum. Her husband was at her side when she died in January 1828, of dropsy, the one man who had stood by her through her eccentric, and sometimes violent, exhibitionism.

MORDAUNT, Lady Harriet 1848–1906

As with a number of young and attractive 'comfortably-off' women during the Victorian era, here was someone who married for financial security rather than love, with rather predictable results. The daughter of Sir Thomas Moncrieffe, Harriet grew up in their wealthy Perth home with fifteen siblings. Her good looks attracted a variety of suitors but she settled for a possessive but rich country squire, Sir Charles Mordaunt, a Conservative MP twelve years her senior. They married in 1866.

While Harriet liked to party and socialise, Charles liked to hunt, shoot and fish, and often left her alone to go on fishing trips, unaware of the number of male visitors during his absences. Returning from one trip unexpectedly in 1869, he found the Prince of Wales, no less, watching Harriet driving her pony-drawn carriage. The Prince had quite a reputation as a philanderer and Charles not only made sure that Bertie, as he was known, made a prompt departure, but also took his revenge on Harriet by arranging for the ponies to be shot while she watched.

Harriet's liaisons continued, a not uncommon lifestyle among bored women of her class. The venue, however, was from hereon not always her own magnificent home in Warwickshire, but rather more seedy hotel rooms and summer-houses. Not unexpectedly, she became pregnant in 1869 and gave birth to a daughter (and not the heir Charles was waiting for), which was unlikely to be her husband's. The baby was born with an eye defect which Harriet seemed to think was a punishment for her indiscretions. She feared the baby would end up blind and that the cause was gonorrhoea. Such fears led her to confess her adulterous relationships to her husband – Lord Cole and Sir Frederic Johnstone on the list along with a continued relationship with the Prince of Wales.

Her husband went on the hunt for revenge again. He sued for divorce almost immediately (1870) naming the Prince as a co-respondent. Her parents, in an attempt to hush up the scandal, persuaded her to enter an asylum. There could be no divorce if she was 'proved' insane. Harriet was taken to court by her husband, who called the Prince of Wales – who denied adultery – as one witness. If he was to be believed, this would prove Harriet a fantasist and indeed insane. Her family and servants also gave evidence of her 'insanity' – e.g. bursting into tears, eating coal and hiding pennies (!).

Even the Prince's own physician testified that Harriet was insane and the divorce case was dismissed at this stage, with Harriet committed.

After various appeals, Charles got his divorce in 1875 but this did not mean that Harriet was no longer regarded as insane. There are many suggestions from diverse sources that Harriet faked her insanity, presumably to 'save' her marriage, but she was to spend over thirty years in a variety of asylums around London. Bad? Wicked? Misunderstood? Or just mad?

PAGE, Damaris c.1615–69

It was not unusual for women like Damaris, born into poverty in the East End, to drift into prostitution while still teenagers, in an effort to make a living. Damaris went on from this to become the most famous of the many brothel keepers around the Ratcliffe Highway, a notorious street on the river at Wapping. Even Samuel Pepys gives her a mention as the 'great bawd of the seamen'.

Damaris, although married in 1640, provided brothels for sailors and it is likely she assisted the British navy with 'recruiting' – in other words, kidnapping. The women she recruited for her brothels were likely to have been drawn from sailors' wives or widows, with no income of their own. More profitable was the import and export of whores, including Venetian women who were known to be experts in the sex trade. Such women were housed in a more expensive brothel nearby, their rates not affordable by ordinary seamen. Up-market customers apparently included the Duke of York. From 1650 onwards she became a property speculator, able to build a number of houses around the Ratcliffe Highway, thanks to the income from the four girls on duty at each of her brothels.

Meanwhile, she had married a second husband (1653) and was tried for bigamy (which was dismissed on the ground of the first marriage being 'unsanctified'), with a second charge of manslaughter. This charge related to an attempted abortion – using an oyster fork – during which her 'patient' died. The result meant she was sentenced to be hanged, but, luckily for Damaris, she was pregnant herself and spent three years in Newgate prison instead, where her (stillborn) child was born – although some sources disagree on this.

The Poor Whores' Petition, 'signed' by Damaris Page.

One of her 'houses' was the first to be targeted in 1668 during the bawdy house riots protesting about the laxness in policing morals, especially when compared with the severity of persecuting religious dissenters. As a result, Damaris put her name (although she was illiterate) to the Poor Whores'

Petition sent to the royal courtesan, Barbara Palmer (Lady Castlemaine), requesting help in rebuilding one of the brothels that had been burnt down. How much help was forthcoming is not known, but business soon resumed.

While sources seem to agree that she died a wealthy woman, the location is not clear. While some creditable sources refer to her dying in her own bed, others mention Marshalsea Prison, the infamous debtors' prison in South London. This latter version of events seems unlikely given her financial status, but …

PRIDDEN, Sarah (known as Sally Salisbury) c.1691–1724

At the age of three, Shrewsbury-born Sally and her family (her father was a bricklayer) moved to the unsavoury (then) St. Giles area of London. At just nine years old, she began working as a seamstress but this was short-lived for no clear reason; though possibly because she was responsible for losing some expensive lace. She tried shelling peas, peeling walnuts, making matches etc until a notorious rake – and convicted rapist – Colonel Charteris took the attractive youngster on as his mistress.

SARAH PRIDDEN,
(alias Sally Salisbury.)

Sarah Pridden. (*Wellcome Images*)

By the time she was fourteen, he had abandoned her and Sally was back in London selling newspapers, until procured by one brothel keeper after another. She was now in demand among the aristocracy as well as the young local apprentices. Her clientele included Lord Bentinck, Lord Bolingbroke, the Earl of Cardigan, the Duke of Buckingham and even, seemingly, the Prince of Wales, who became King George II. She re-invented herself as Sally Salisbury and claimed to be a member of that titled family, denying her humble origins, but still ended up in prison a few times, though not for long as some gent was always around to bail her out. Legend has it that in one case in 1713, even the judge sanctioned her release to avail himself of her favours, incurring him a reprimand for corruption.

She certainly acquired a reputation for being fiery as well as vivacious and attractive. One of her biographers (and there have been several, the earliest volume in the British Library pre-dating her death!) tells of her stealing £20 in gold from a 'wealthy Dutchman' who she treated with contempt in spite of his generosity and of her returning to Charteris for a while; he even fought a duel over her. Another writes about her getting the Earl of Cardigan drunk at Newmarket races and stealing his clothes and jewels – which he luckily treated as a joke.

It was Sally's quick temper that sealed her fate in the end. While at the Three Tuns in Covent Garden just before Christmas in 1722, she became angered that the Hon. John Finch, another lover, had given opera tickets to her sister and not to her – and stabbed him. She was charged with attempted murder and although Finch tried hard to have the charges dropped she was found guilty at the Old Bailey. The sentence was a fine of £100 and one year in prison with a further two years suspended. The prison conditions at Bridewell (for vagrant women) were appalling, in spite of her many male visitors lavishing her with gifts to make her more comfortable. There was a sadistic inspector who was responsible for caning her – amongst others – whenever she ceased working at one of the imposed labours such as beating hemp (per Hogarth's famous paintings), and her health quickly deteriorated.

Although transferred to Newgate, Sally did not survive the year. She died there from what was then described as 'gaol fever' (typhus) but which most sources refer to as syphilis. This prostitute-turned-courtesan-of-a-sort was popular to the end, and her funeral coffin was followed by four coaches.

SAND, George 1804–76

Born Armandine Aurore Lucie Dupin in Paris, this famous novelist was brought up by her mother and grand-mother until fourteen when she joined a convent, more as an escape than as a devotee. She was a disruptive influence and was soon recalled, and is alleged to have seduced her first lover (a neighbour) before reaching the age of seventeen. An eccentric tutor fuelled her desire for liberation, encouraging her to wear men's clothing while riding horseback.

Married at nineteen to the son of a baron, she became disillusioned by his coarseness which did not sit well with her idea of love and, after the birth of their son, she began to look for new conquests. When she left her husband to move back to Paris (seemingly taking her newly born daughter, but not her son), after ensuring she was going to receive an allowance from him, this in itself caused quite a scandal. The long-standing affair she began with a charming young writer, Jules Sandeau, prompted her change of name to Sand – with George a nod to the fact that,

George Sand.

with her intention of being a writer, it did not pay to be a woman.

George and Jules gradually drifted apart, she wearying of his jealousy, leaving her to pursue another younger writer, the poet Alfred de Musset, while attracting many other admirers. Their admiration was for her burgeoning success as a writer and for her iconoclastic approach to life – she still wore men's clothes, she had taken to smoking cigars in public (shock, horror) and was an early proponent of women's liberation. She is said to have had at least one sexual relationship with a woman, the actress Marie Duval, leading to accusations of lesbianism.

Alfred was followed by an Italian doctor, a French lawyer, a Swiss poet (challenged to a duel in defence of her literary honour!) and, most famously, the composer Frederic Chopin. Apparently she had tried to seduce Franz Liszt before turning her attention to Chopin, while involved with the French playwright Felicien Mallefille. As with her other lovers, they were both a number of years younger, but George decided that Chopin, who was initially rather disapproving, was a better match for her intellect. They were both internationally famous by now and she continued to write (romantic, passionate novels) after they fled to Majorca, where the consumptive Chopin worked on a number of his preludes.

Chopin's health – not helped by an apparent opium addiction – deteriorated to such an extent that George travelled with him back to her home in Nohant, a French village. Here is where he wrote his funeral march, among other famous compositions; she was writing more political works during this period (1840s). However, when Chopin spent time in Paris, he believed stories of George's infidelity (which could of course have been true …) and the relationship broke up – after nine years – leaving them both apparently devastated. He died in 1849, her last lover, although many younger men 'visited' her at Nohant during her final decades, a number of whom provided her with the sex life she still craved.

While not a conventional beauty, the scandalous George Sand attracted men into old age because of her lewd outlook on life, her sense of humour, and her devil-may-care attitude. The author of over forty novels, and many plays, she died surrounded by children and grand-children at Nohant. Boring, she wasn't.

Chapter Three

Serial Killers

BÁTHORY, Countess Elizabeth 1560–1614

Separating fact from fiction is not easy when it comes to the legendary Elizabeth Báthory. She certainly came from a comfortable background, brought up as a Calvinist, her family virtually ruling Transylvania when the area was part of Hungary. Her arranged marriage, at fourteen, was not unusual, but more apocryphal is the prior murder of the lover who fathered her illegitimate baby. If she indeed gave the order for her husband-to-be to have the lover castrated and torn to pieces by dogs, then her later reputation would not be out of keeping.

Elizabeth Báthory.

The Countess acquired the reputation of enjoying sadistically torturing and killing young girls, usually servants from peasant stock, whose parents did not make a fuss when their daughters went missing. There are graphic accounts of the tortures she instigated, aided and abetted by her favoured, older, servants. These include burning with a variety of red-hot metals, beatings, biting, piercing of lips and under fingernails with needles, starvation, whipping and stabbing. With a childhood nurse said to have practised black magic, a devil-worshipping uncle and an aunt regarded as a witch, it is not difficult to see where her influences lie.

After her husband, the aristocratic Hungarian Ferenc Nádasdy, died in 1604, he left enormous debts. A few years later, for financial reasons and partly perhaps for other more unsavoury reasons, the Countess opened a school to teach etiquette to a superior class of local girl, because she was now finding it difficult to recruit from peasant stock, who had presumably got wind of her activities. The noble families were not as gullible as their proletariat predecessors, however, and did not turn a blind eye to the stories emanating from the Duchess's impressive residence, Csejte Castle in the village of Čachtice (whose remains, now in Western Slovakia, can still be visited). As a result, and with the apparent support of a local Lutheran minister, angry fathers and brothers from noble families were behind the Castle being investigated by local authorities, who found the injured and dead bodies of young women on the premises. Elizabeth and her accomplices were arrested, but her social standing meant she was not put on trial. Thirty witnesses came forward at the trial of her accomplices, where the number of victims was assessed at over 600, seemingly listed in a journal belonging to the Countess. Her accomplices were found guilty, collectively, of killing eighty girls, and subsequently executed in the grisly fashion of the time, but she was shut away in her castle, in solitary confinement, dying there in 1614.

The stories of the Countess bathing in, and drinking, her victims' blood in vampiric fashion, seem to have been added at a later date, with an emphasis on the anti-ageing process of virgins' blood in particular. She has become the stuff of legend, and no doubt some of the stories of her activities have been exaggerated, with even the trial records at some variance. What happened to her own seven children is also impossible to establish. But, certainly, she deserves her reputation as the world's most prolific serial killer.

BORDEN, Lizzie 1860–1927

Lizzie Borden took an axe
And gave her mother forty whacks.
When she saw what she had done
She gave her father forty-one …

So the rhyme goes. This was a high profile case in the United States at the time, with few non-locals doubting that Lizzie was guilty of murdering her father and stepmother, in spite of the non-guilty verdict. It was high profile because she was a part of the wealthy elite in the up-market city of Fall River, who defended their own. The judge and the prosecuting team could not be seen to have any doubts about the innocence of someone of her social standing.

Lizzie Borden, from Marshall & Cavendish Murder Casebook 1990

Lizzie's childhood was apparently unhappy: a 'mean' (in spite of his wealth) father, a stepmother (from 1862) to whom she hardly spoke and to whom she and her older sister referred as 'Mrs Borden' because they wanted to distance themselves from someone who they were convinced was after their father's fortune. In 1892, Lizzie 'discovered' the body of her butchered father in the sitting room, and called to the maid, who was upstairs, to fetch a doctor. The doctor had no doubt that the first of more than ten blows from a hatchet had killed him. When the stepmother was then sought out and found upstairs, with twice as many wounds, the police investigation became a media sensation.

Lizzie was the obvious suspect – her sister was out of town, she stood to inherit a fortune, she kept changing her mind about her movements during that fatal morning, and, during the week between the crimes and her arrest, she had been witnessed burning some 'soiled' clothing … Initially, she was vilified in the press, but, during the year before the trial came to court, there was enough time for her to collect plenty of support, coming across as a religious woman who was a God-fearing Sunday school teacher, incapable of such bestiality.

Although the hatchet used was found (before fingerprinting or DNA of course), there was no forensic evidence provided by the prosecution. The fact that Lizzie had attempted, unsuccessfully, to buy prussic acid (a restricted substance) from the local drug-store the day before the murders was excluded from the evidence. Similarly, the fact that the transfer of the deeds of one of the Borden properties to Abby, the step-mother, was due to take place on the day of the murder did not come to light until after the trial. So, in spite of Lizzie's erratic and unconvincing account of her movements, the all-male jury were won over by the expensive defence lawyer's appeal to their sense of chivalry: 'Gentlemen, does she look like a fiend?' They took just ninety minutes to find her not guilty.

The sisters inherited their father's huge fortune, but they never married, and died within days of each other in 1927. No further scandal was attached to Lizzie – but nor was any-one else ever charged with the murders.

CIANCIULLI, Leonarda 1893–1970

Leonarda had a hard time as a child in Italy, born to a rape victim, and did not do much better as an adult, serving several years in prison for fraud. She married during the First World War but only four of her seventeen pregnancies were successful; three miscarried, and ten children died while very young. In 1930, she and her husband lost their home during an earthquake and moved away, giving Leonarda the opportunity to start up a business – a small shop selling clothing with a profitable sideline in fortune telling. Her husband turned to alcohol and left the family home.

The neighbours and customers regarded Leonarda as a kind, helpful type who, in spite of her own problems, could offer them potions to help with theirs. What they did not know was that, for religious or superstitious reasons, Leonarda seems to have been convinced that she could only save her three sons from being killed in the Second World War by offering human sacrifices in their place. So, when the eldest was called up, she persuaded one customer (Faustina Setti, who was looking for the man of her dreams) to drink a drug-laced wine before using an axe on her body.

Leonarda then made the decision which places her as more than just a killer. She boiled the woman's remains with caustic soda, producing a mush which she found to serve as an acceptable soap. The left over blood was mixed with the ingredients she used for tea cakes which she served to her customers and this was said to add a distinct flavour. Even her sons apparently appreciated them. No doubt.

The same routine – drugged wine, the axe, the pot – followed for the next victim (Francesca Soavi, who was trying to find work), and for her third (Virginia Cacioppo, an opera singer whose career was flagging) she discovered that by adding a bottle of cologne to the mix the soap was creamy and more saleable. Leonarda's memoirs mention the particular sweetness of Virginia's blood compared to the other women, but it was Virginia's death that was her downfall, because her family would not believe that she would just disappear without telling anyone where she had gone and she had been seen going into Leonarda's home.

A police investigation found plenty of evidence in Leonarda's kitchen, and this 'doting mother' confessed all. She was tried for murder in 1946 but was completely unrepentant, convinced that she had done what any mother would do to save her sons. Sentenced to thirty years, the Deadly Soap-Maker of Correggio, as she became known, died in prison in 1970 from a brain haemorrhage.

COTTON, Mary Ann 1832–73

Mary Ann Cotton, nee Robson, has gone down in history as Britain's most prolific serial killer of the nineteenth century, earning her the soubriquet of Black Widow. This, however, was the daughter of a miner with a Christian upbringing, from a quiet English village. From the age of eight, when her father, the breadwinner, died, Mary Ann had a dread of the workhouse and gradually became aware that her good looks could secure her some security by way of a husband.

When she became pregnant in 1852 by the besotted William Mowbray, they married secretly and moved to Plymouth, but five children in as many years and a husband working away meant that her struggles continued. Another four children followed and all were insured with the Prudential for Mary Ann's peace of mind. Just as well, because seven died in infancy, a high rate even at a time of high infant mortality, and William too died of a 'gastric complaint' in 1865. The Pru happily paid out each time, providing Mary Ann with a good income.

An eighth child died and the ninth was sent to Mary Ann's mother, leaving her free to find employment as a nurse where she could find herself another besotted husband-to-be, George Ward, who became husband number two – but only after he had also taken out adequate insurance a year before his death in 1866. Other deaths followed in quick succession, after she had taken on a job as housekeeper to widower James Robinson (she was back up North by now). First his baby daughter died with yet another gastric complaint and then Mary Ann's mother. Although there was no insurance pay-out for the latter, she was able to sell her mother's furniture to get hold of some cash before marrying James.

More gastric complaints killed off Mary Ann's remaining daughter and one of James's children, each succeeded by a cheque from the Pru. It was James, and not the Pru, who at last started piecing things together. He survived, as the only husband not to take out life insurance. In fact, he threw her out – into the arms of Frederick Cotton and his sister in Northumberland, family friends. The sister died after yet another gastric attack, and Frederick (who she married bigamously in 1870, young Charlie being born in 1871) followed when she decided their lodger, Joseph Nattrass, was a better catch. The lodger was superseded in turn by John Quick-Manning (there is some dispute re the name here – he may have been Richard Quick Mann), a customs and excise officer who was socially superior. Mary Ann 'nursed' him during his recovery from smallpox but, although she had his child, he and his children were all dead within the year.

Finally, a doctor refused to sign the death certificate for the last of Mary Ann's relatives to die, seven-year-old Charlie Cotton, until an inquest had been carried out, because he had seen the boy alive and well the previous day. The arsenic found in his stomach led to the exhumation of other suspected victims, all of whom were similarly contaminated. Unbelievably, it seems that the Pru may have paid out again, though accounts do vary.

The evidence against Mary Ann was overwhelming, although the trial for murder of Charlie and five others was delayed by her twelfth pregnancy; some historians have disputed the number of pregnancies, but twelve is the general consensus. Stubbornly, she continued to maintain her innocence. However, it only took the jury ninety minutes to decide she was guilty and she was convicted at Durham Assizes and sentenced to death. Her execution became headline news because of the bungling way it was carried out, leaving her dangling so that she took several minutes to choke to death.

Retribution for her twenty years of killing was partly delayed by her moving around and by her name changes, but this was probably not deliberate avoidance on her part. She seemed to have had no qualms about what she had done; some have blamed her actions on the ready availability of arsenic in Victorian Britain, but that doesn't mean she had to use it …

'Mary Ann Cotton – she's dead and she's rotten' so the rhyme goes. Quite.

DYER, Amelia c.1838–96

Apart from her mother's mental health issues, Amelia came from a pretty normal family living near Bristol. Her father was a shoemaker and she had four siblings, all of whom could read and write. She trained as a corset maker and married George Thomas, a much older man, in 1861, training as a nurse during her brief marriage; he died in 1869.

Amelia Dyer.

Then, as now, nurses were not well paid and Amelia discovered a more profitable niche. She opened a 'house of confinement' in a Bristol suburb taking in unmarried women who were about to give birth and disposing of – usually stifling – the unwanted babies for a handsome fee. She also fostered babies for a weekly fee, using laudanum to curb their appetite and their cries, but even this was not enough. It was more lucrative to charge a one-off payment to fully adopt such babies and she could then strangle and dump them promptly, at no cost. This also avoided questions from the NSPCC (formed in 1884) or serving any further prison sentences for child neglect, which apparently did happen to her early on.

This routine went on for several decades, surprisingly for us in the twenty-first century but not so surprisingly in the nineteenth. She moved around the country quite a few times and changed her name, advertising her services under various aliases:

> 'Married Couple with no family, would adopt healthy child, nice country home. £10. Harding, c/o Ship's Letter Exchange, Stoke's Croft, Bristol.'

Amelia also responded to advertisements such as the one placed by Evelina Marmon in January 1896, 'Wanted respectable woman to take young child.' Evelina handed over her £10 and Amelia took the baby to Willesden, her address at the time, where apparently her grown up daughter, Polly (in her twenties) helped her to strangle baby Doris and take her by train to the riverside at Reading. By this time at least seven small bodies, strangled with white tape, had been found in the Thames by bargemen who had contacted the police. A faded address was found on some of the wrapping used. This address, in Caversham (the Reading area) was linked to Amelia, and the Willesden house was searched, revealing telegrams and letters about adoption. Worse than that was the stench of rotting flesh in the house, although no human remains were found.

Poor Evelina was asked to see if she could identify her baby, just eleven days after handing her over to Amelia and identify her she did. But Reading police found evidence of at least twenty babies entrusted to Amelia's 'care' in the previous two months alone. Imagine how many she had 'removed' over some thirty years, although some sources do suggest that she spent a lot of her earlier years, post marriage, in the workhouse. This is borne out by a record of her stealing a knife from a workhouse near Bristol in June 1895.

She tried to commit suicide when arrested at her last address in Reading. Around the same time, she managed to get her daughter and son-in-law off the hook and confess that the police would know her victims by the white tape around their necks. She was charged with the murder of just one baby, Doris Marmon, and tried at the Old Bailey. One baby was all it took. Her daughter actually gave evidence for the prosecution and the jury needed little more than five minutes to find her guilty – her plea of insanity was rejected out of hand.

Baby farming, as it was called, did not stop with Amelia's execution (at Newgate), but it did decline substantially. She was the oldest woman to be executed for over fifty years. While not the only baby farmer tried and convicted, she must surely have been the most prolific.

Postscript: In the macabre collection at London's Crime Museum is Amelia's execution rope, a knife she stole from Barton Regis Workhouse, and a letter to a mother of a child in her care.

EDMUNDS, Christiana 1829–1907

A third option arises for this particular female; wicked or misunderstood or insane? Her father was said to have had a mental illness, her brother died in an asylum, a sister probably committed suicide; an early example of what would now be described as a dysfunctional family.

The family were, however, definitely middle class, with Christiana educated at a private school. She grew up in Margate and moved to a grand house in Brighton with her mother and sister in the 1860s. It seems that it wasn't until she was forty that she fell in love; with a neighbour, Dr Charles Beard, but he was married. He did not reciprocate her feelings, but he did reply to the affectionate letters she sent him, although in a restrained fashion. Christiana did not give up easily; she presented his wife with a gift of poisoned chocolate creams, but these only made her sick. Dr Beard, though, sent Christiana packing.

Brighton then became the epi-centre of poisoned sweets and chocolates which turned up in a number of shops, causing a number of people to fall ill, and one four-year-old to die. Strychnine was found in the chocolates, but although Christiana appeared as a witness at the inquest, it was to state that she had also eaten similar sweets and become ill. At this point, she was trying to lay the 'blame' on Maynards, a well-known Brighton confectioners.

Christiana then changed her modus operandi, sending parcels of poisoned fruit and cakes to a variety of individuals, including Mrs Beard. The plum cake in her parcel was tasted by her suspicious servants, at least one of whom fell ill. The Chief Constable placed an advertisement in the local newspaper offering a reward for information and Dr Beard went to the police, who matched Christiana's handwriting to the labels on the parcels.

Such was the interest in the Chocolate Cream Murderer that it was decided that she might not have a fair trial in Brighton, and she was moved to Newgate Prison and tried at the Old Bailey in January 1872. There she was charged with the murder of the four-year-old, Sidney Barker. No motive was given for the randomness of the poisonings, but it seems a drastic way of trying to cover up the attempted murder of Mrs Beard, if that – as some suggest – was indeed the reason. The prosecution did find evidence of Christiana sending boys to the shops (mainly Maynards) to buy chocolates which she injected with strychnine and then left lying around or returned, apparently untouched, to the naïve shopkeeper. Strychnine, like arsenic, was readily available from the local chemist in those days.

The defence was insanity but the jury were unconvinced and she was convicted and sentenced to death, attempting that Victorian ploy of announcing she was pregnant to try and avoid the sentence, easily proved false by a medical examination. However, the Home Seretary overturned the jury's decision, deciding that she was not guilty 'by reason of insanity'.

Christiana was transferred to Broadmoor at the age of forty-three, at which time she was described as very vain with false hair and heavy make-up. It seems she enjoyed dances given for the patients but her prime pleasure was in causing mischief – provoking arguments, passing notes, hiding possessions. Although quiet and 'trusted' she was regarded as a danger to the public and ended her days in Broadmoor.

GUNNESS, Belle 1859 – ? (vanished April 1908)

Here is a woman who never got her come-uppance. A striking six-foot tall stone-mason's daughter, born in Norway, she followed her sister to the USA in around 1882 in search of riches. She married a Swede, Mads Sorensen, in 1884, producing two children who died, after they had been insured; some sources argue that their deaths were much later and yet others argue about the number of children, if any, and the dates of their deaths. In 1900 her husband also died 'of heart failure' with two hefty insurance pay-outs, enabling her to buy a farm in Indiana.

Belle married Peter Gunness soon after and promptly insured him, too. He died within the year when a sausage grinder fell on his head and his baby daughter also died inexplicably. Belle found that she could find further wealthy men through advertising, e.g. 'Comely widow … [with] large farm … desires to make the acquaintance of a gentleman … with a view to joining fortunes …' This way, she attracted a stream of men, most of them young, all bringing cash per her request, but all apparently charmed by Belle's seductive wiles – and her cooking. They all disappeared not long after their arrival, however, explained away by Belle as visitors from the 'old country'. In the meantime, she had her handyman, Ray Lamphere, to keep her company in bed.

It was probably not a coincidence that her farmhouse caught fire in April 1908 soon after a brother of one of the missing men had started making enquiries. Andrew Helgelein – surname spellings vary – had responded to an ad in a Norwegian-language newspaper. His brother knew where Andrew was going and that he had taken as much as $3,000 cash with him, so he travelled to Indiana to investigate, only to find a burned out ruin, with men digging up body after body in the debris. Andrew's dismembered body was just one of them.

At least fourteen bodies (perhaps as many as forty, quite possibly more) were pieced together, the use of quicklime not helping, and there were finds of men's watches and human teeth. A few bodies were those of children; one female corpse could have been assumed to be Belle's as it remained unidentified although most of the others had relatives come forward once the finds started being reported in the press. The unidentified female, however, was missing a head and of a much slighter build than the rather stout forty-eight-year-old Belle.

The local sheriff insisted on arresting Ray Lamphere for Belle's (and other) murders. He was acquitted of murder but not of arson, for which he received a prison sentence, dying there (of tuberculosis). While in prison, he had spoken of Belle being the guilty party and of burying bodies for her after she had cut them up. The headless woman was apparently a vagrant Belle had picked up before setting fire to the house and then disappearing with the money that so many naïve men had 'invested'.

So this was one woman who, literally, got away with murder on a grand scale.

HAHN, Anna 1906–38

It seems that those immigrants arriving in the USA before the Second World War – or even much earlier – did find fame and fortune, but only by breaking the law, even venturing into murder. Anna Hahn was one of these and she is selected for inclusion here at random from amongst many.

She first found work with relatives in the States in around 1929, but, once married to Philip Hahn, they opened a small bakery – until he became ill following an excessive consumption of croton oil, a fierce purgative, administered by his wife. In the meantime, Anna had become popular at the

German beer gardens in Cincinnati, singing Bavarian ballads and clinking glasses with her admirers, none in their first flush of youth. As many of these elderly men were in need of care, Anna began to offer her services as a 'nurse' and her reward, as they died one by one, was to be named in their wills.

There were plenty of gullible 'patients' who regarded her as an angel of mercy, one of whom, Jacob Wagner, was only in her care for some twenty-four hours before dying. When he, and another, days later, both died with similar diagnoses – stomach pains and vomiting – the local Police Chief was called in. An autopsy on Wagner revealed the presence of poison, and several other bodies were exhumed as a result, with arsenic and croton oil featuring prominently. At least five elderly men fell foul of this angel of mercy, leaving her thousands of dollars, and, in one case, a house. One man did have a lucky escape when he noticed the flies on his beer glass keeling over – he asked Anna to drink from the glass but she refused, so ending her employment.

When Hahn was questioned, she denied wishing to harm such 'dear old gentlemen' but a quantity of poison found in her home was pretty damning, with her fate sealed when her husband told the police she had been stealing prescription forms and sending their son to fetch poisonous prescriptions. He had become suspicious and refused to take out an insurance as suggested by his wife, although he suspected she had attempted to poison him anyway, a reference to his earlier illness.

In spite of her emotional appeals during her trial, talking of her 'poor darlings' whom she had comforted and tickled as they neared their end, she was convicted. During the trial, there was some emphasis on her gambling habit, which may well have prompted her actions, giving her a motive other than sheer greed. She became the first woman to die in the electric chair in the state of Ohio.

KING, Jessie 1861–89

Born in Glasgow, Jessie lived a blameless life in local mills and an Edinburgh laundry until becoming homeless and pregnant around 1887. She was taken in by Thomas Pearson, a fifty-nine-year-old labourer who may or may not have been the father of her unborn child. It may also be that Jessie had been prostituting herself by this time.

Jessie's baby died soon after birth but the 'couple' saw a newspaper advertisement for a baby boy who was being put up for adoption and brought home the baby she wanted. No doubt they also acquired a fee for so doing – legal at the time. However, motherhood obviously turned out to be less attractive than Jessie had envisaged, and her 'husband' (in name only) came home one day to find the boy had been 'put into a home'.

There was no investigation into the baby's absence – why would there be? But in October 1888, the body of another baby was discovered on waste ground by schoolboys who had randomly kicked open the parcel he was concealed in. Most local residents were upset, even tearful, at the discovery, which *was* investigated by the police, but not 'Mrs Pearson', whose landlord recalled taking in a baby girl who had disappeared. It seems he was told that this baby had been sold on, not an unusual occurrence at the time. While not the same baby, the police were curious about this latter incident, and a search of the Pearson household revealed the body of a baby girl wrapped in canvas.

The two dead babies had similar ligature wounds around the throats, but in fact forensics were unnecessary as Jessie made a full confession, apparently to escape the death sentence. As for Pearson, he turned Queen's evidence, helping to convict her, and was rewarded with immunity for being a Crown witness.

Jessie was found guilty of the two murders, with a unanimous verdict from the jury after less than five minutes and she was also no doubt guilty of killing the boy who had been 'put into a home' but in fact had 'disappeared' but in this case there was no body. There were also suspicions that she had in fact been involved in other cases of baby farming, taking money to look after babies and then killing them. Such babies were usually illegitimate.

When the judge announced that Jessie would hang, the only baby farmer to receive such a sentence in Scotland, she fainted. Press coverage gave her no mercy, with no reference to her vulnerability or the fact that she may have had mental health issues. It does seem, incidentally, that she had a surviving child at some point, because there are newspaper reports of her saying a last goodbye to her son, Thomas.

Jessie made several attempts at suicide before seemingly resigning herself to her fate, and was taken to the gallows on 11 March 1889, the last woman to be hanged in Edinburgh. The first delegated executioner declined the job of hanging a woman, but it was not difficult to find a replacement and Jessie was buried in an unmarked grave within the walls of Calton prison (now a car park), many hundreds waiting outside for news of her death, indicated by the flying of a black flag.

MARTI, Enriqueta 1868–1913

Here is one straightforward case where there can surely be no doubt as to whether she was misunderstood or just plain evil. A kidnapper and murderer of children, a procuress for paedophiles, and sometimes also described as a 'witch doctor', Enriqueta arrived in Barcelona (the pornography capital of Europe at the time) in the late nineteenth century where she could see that working as a nanny and servant did not pay as well as prostitution. Not surprisingly, her choice of 'profession' caused her 1895 marriage to an obscure painter to fail.

Enriqueta Marti, shown here with victims Teresita and Angelica.

Enriqueta, whose early life is undocumented, opened a brothel in 1909 and served a short spell in prison, her release secured no doubt by one of her wealthy clients. Her brothel became more shocking, more macabre, than any other, however, in that she – dressed in rags – wandered the destitute areas of Barcelona, selecting apparently abandoned children that she kidnapped to serve as prostitutes. In the evenings, dressed in contrastingly luxurious outfits, she frequented wealthy venues such as the casinos, offering these children to likely 'gentlemen'.

She had an even more horrifying scheme to obtain money from wealthy women. For these, she murdered children – presumably those who were not earning her money as prostitutes – from infants up to the age of twelve. These children provided fat, blood, hair and bones all of which could be turned into beauty treatments and elixirs, with young blood regarded as good for long life and young fat good to conserve young skin. Her reputation as a witch-doctor came from the extra trade in potions for such then-incurable diseases such as tuberculosis and syphilis. Rich women may have guessed at the source of these products, but with poor children regarded pretty much as vermin, this would not have made any difference.

Her lucrative and nauseating career came to an end in 1912, thanks to a nosy neighbour who had seen a stream of young girls entering Enriqueta's flat. Detectives were called in – bearing in mind that there was a long list of missing children that they were investigating – and found two girls who gave horrific accounts of witnessing other children being starved and murdered. Forensic experts searched this flat and others she had lived in and found the remains of at least twelve different bodies, with other unidentified remains. They also found blood-soaked clothes, a knife, macabre 'recipe' books and jars of human remains including children's hair.

The Vampire of Barcelona, as she became known, was arrested, but never tried. While awaiting trial in prison, with the horrified general public calling for her to be garrotted, she was beaten to death by fellow prisoners who were just as horrified. This nasty piece of work was buried secretly in a common grave – did anyone mourn her passing? It seems unlikely.

ROBINSON, Sarah Jane c.1838–1906

Although she became known as the Massachusetts Borgia, Sarah was actually born in Ireland. Her family emigrated when she was fourteen and she married a factory worker five years later, producing eight children, five surviving, stretching the family's limited finances so that they were constantly on the move to avoid debt collectors.

In 1881, her landlord died of 'heart disease' after several thousand dollars went missing from his apartment, and Sarah promptly paid off her debts. Debts kept spiralling, although Sarah earned some money as a dressmaker but fraudulently re-mortgaging the same property over and over again to raise money. The next death was that of her husband, Moses, with a $2,000 insurance payout from The Order of Pilgrim Fathers. Another $4,000 was paid out when her sister and brother in law died a year later … closely followed by her ten-year-old daughter and latterly her even younger niece and nephew.

Not surprisingly, the insurance company's suspicions were aroused when two more of Sarah's children died. She was finally arrested for the murder of her son, William, thanks to a suspicious doctor who had analysed William's vomit and discussed the finding of arsenic with the Boston police chief. The Order of Pilgrim Fathers now persuaded the police to exhume the bodies of other relatives insured by Sarah, all of whom were found to have died of arsenic poisoning.

Initially, Sarah – who had, incidentally, a number of oblivious suitors – was tried for the murder of William, thanks to American procedures and there was also a suggestion that she had been aided by an accomplice, Thomas Smith, a possible lover. The case against Smith was dismissed, and Sarah's six-day trial resulted in a hung jury, who had deliberated for forty-eight hours.

The following year, 1888, she was charged with four more murders and this time she was found guilty and sentenced to hang. Astonishingly, a petition with 500 signatures – including some jury members! – appealed for her sentence to be commuted to life imprisonment, suggesting she had more charisma than her appearance suggested. The appeal was granted, with the proviso that the sentence should be spent in solitary confinement. Sarah remained self-possessed throughout the investigations and trials, although at one point early on she did try the classic 'insane' defence. Resigned to her fate, the only woman in solitary confinement in Massachusetts died in prison on Christmas Eve 1906 following a prolonged illness.

SHERMAN, Lydia 1824–78

Raised by her uncle after she was orphaned, Lydia was working as a seamstress when she met a widower at her church, marrying him when she was seventeen. Edward Struck was a New York police officer and they had six children in seven years before he lost his job after a dispute involving a detective who was killed when Edward was AWOL. He seems to have become a burden for Lydia, but soon died a mysterious but timely death after Lydia had bought some rat poison and had taken out insurance on his life …

While subsequently working as a nurse, three of Lydia's (insured!) children and her two stepchildren died, conveniently relieving some of her financial difficulties. With no suspicions attached to the deaths, Lydia moved to Connecticut. There, more help came along in the form of a wealthy farmer and fisherman, much older than Lydia but ideal husband material, until such time as she tired of him. He died shortly after changing his will in her favour, regarding her as a doting wife.

Still unsuspected, Lydia applied for a job as housekeeper to another widower (also with children) and they married in 1870 after she had been working for him for just a few months. Horatio (or Nelson in some sources) Sherman was a heavy drinker, who mixed baking soda in his cider to make it foam. When he too lost his life, soon after two of his children had also become sick and died, the blame was put on a mix up of the products, the baking soda and arsenic stored side by side. But this time, at last, suspicions were aroused.

Having found arsenic in Horatio's body, a local physician arranged for exhumations of the Sherman children and of her previous husband. All were indeed poisoned. Lydia finally stood trial in 1872 and was initially found guilty of the second-degree murder of her third husband, the evidence being circumstantial. However, she confessed while on remand to murdering her previous husbands and 'four' children. Unsurprisingly, she was sentenced to life in prison in 1873, although that in itself was lenient in the circumstances – but the story does not end there.

Lydia escaped from prison in 1877 having feigned an 'enfeebling' illness, and thanks to the negligence of a careless member of staff, probably the Matron. She may not have been re-captured had she not given two different names to the manager of a hotel in Rhode Island. Raising his suspicions, she was returned to prison. But not for long. She died there in 1878 after a brief – this time genuine – illness. Her confessions were published soon after, and she has been described as a Modern Lucrezia Borgia and The Queen of Poisoners. It is believed that she killed ten family members – or more – and not just the seven she admitted to.

WADDINGHAM, Dorothea 1899–1936

Little is known of Dorothea's childhood, apart from the fact that she was apparently brought up on a farm. But it is known that she was convicted in her twenties and early thirties several times – for fraud and petty theft while married to an elderly husband who died of cancer in 1930.

In 1935, given her straitened circumstances, she and Ronald Sullivan, her new husband, decided to open a nursing home in Nottingham. Dorothea became 'matron' with Ronald an assistant, although her only experience was helping out in the ward at Burton-on-Trent workhouse.

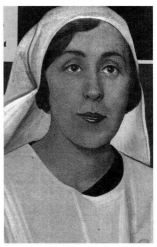

Dorothea Waddingham, from Marshall & Cavendish Murder Casebook 1990.

Two patients recommended to the home by a nursing association – eighty-nine-year-old Mrs Baguley and her daughter, Ada, fifty, who had 'creeping paralysis' – came to an agreement with Dorothea in January 1935. In exchange for their care in the home Mrs Baguley would leave the matron her estate, worth some £1,600. In May, Mrs Baguley had a stroke, apparently, and died six days after re-writing her will, but no suspicions were attached to her death, given her age.

However, when her daughter died four months later (cardiovascular degeneration) an odd letter was sent from Dorothea to the Nottingham medical health officer – it seemed to be from Ada requesting that she be cremated and her relatives not informed regarding her death. This rang enough alarm bells to generate a post-mortem, which revealed morphine in the corpse. Mrs Baguley was then exhumed, and more fatal morphine was found. Matron and her lover were arrested and charged with Ada's murder, although the case against Ronald was dismissed due to lack of evidence even though it seems he wrote Ada's note.

In February 1936, the jury found Dorothea guilty, because her claim that she was following doctor's orders had been denied by the clinic's doctor, who had only prescribed morphine for a completely different woman. Her case had not been helped by the large meal she had given Ada, revealed by the post mortem, which seemed to be an attempt to disguise the morphine in her system.

A recommendation for mercy, partly due to Dorothea having four young children, the youngest of whom she was still breast-feeding, was ignored by the judge and by the Home Secretary. Dorothea was hanged in Winson Green Prison, Birmingham, in April, confessing to the two murders before being hanged. Interestingly, the execution was carried out by Thomas Pierrepoint, ably assisted by his nephew, Albert, who subsequently became far more famous.

WILSON, Mary 1893–1962

Mary's notoriety came later in life than most. As a working class domestic who married John Knowles, her Tyneside employer's eldest son, she settled into a staid domestic life. When they took in a lodger, however, and he became her lover, their lives became less routine than most, with the arrangement continuing long term.

Her strong, fit husband became ill in July 1955 and died within just a few weeks, prompting Mary to move to a larger home, accompanied by her lodger, John Russell. But by the end of the same year, he, too, was seriously ill with a bout of stomach cramps. Although 'cared for' by Mary, he died in January and was followed by another lodger that summer.

The new lodger was Oliver Leonard, a retired estate agent in his seventies. He and Mary married in September but Mary called in the doctor just two weeks later because Oliver 'had died in the night'. As the doctor had seen him previously because of a bad cold and had regarded him as frail, he had no qualms about signing the death certificate. There were only small amounts of money (no more than £50) inherited on each occasion by Mary, but it is not known if she had been expecting rather more.

In 1957, Mary married yet again, Ernest Wilson being another retiree in his seventies and another husband that lasted just two weeks! This time she benefited from inheriting his bungalow and an insurance payout. Unsurprisingly, the gossip started, with wedding guests recalling that Mary had joked that leftover wedding cake would come in handy for the funeral

… This was one of the reasons she became known as the Merry Widow of Windy Nook (the family home); there was also the story of her joking with the undertakers about her entitlement to a discount because of the amount of work she was sending their way.

She had evaded suspicion until then because her husbands had left her so little in the way of an inheritance and also because of her age and her previous good character. But now the police decided to exhume the four bodies. All of them contained phosphorus and wheatgerm, the ingredients of a popular rat and cockroach poison. Mary stood trial for the murder of her last two husbands, as the earlier bodies had deteriorated and offered less convincing forensic evidence. The only real defence offered in court was that there was an aphrodisiac containing these ingredients which could have been purchased by an older husband on his marriage … but no such tablets were found and the jury were not convinced.

Mary was found guilty. Although killing one person had been removed from the list of capital crimes by the 1957 Homicide Act, more than one murder meant that she could be, and was, sentenced to death, the last woman in Durham so treated. On appeal, with her age in her favour, this was commuted to life imprisonment. Life however, for her, was just a few more years in Holloway prison where she died, aged seventy.

Chapter Four

'One Off' Killers

BLANDY, Mary 1720–52

Rather foolishly, Mary's middle-class and moneyed father, a lawyer in Henley-on-Thames, advertised a dowry of £10,000 to attract a future husband for his twenty-six-year-old daughter. This did indeed attract the attention of a large number of suitors, but unfortunately Mary's choice was an already married officer in the marines, William Henry Cranstoun. The couple quickly became lovers, in spite of her father's objections, suggesting Mary's naivety rather than, perhaps, her passion.

Mary Blandy.

All accounts of the Mary Blandy affair indicate that she gave her father regular doses of arsenic as suggested by her lover. Her claim that she was unaware that what she administered was poison but was supposed to be a potion to put paid to her father's objections to her lover, is difficult to accept. For a start, some of the servants also ended up with symptoms of arsenic poisoning should they eat any of Mr Blandy's leftover tea or gruel.

Even her father, Francis, suspected that he was being slowly poisoned and broached the subject with Mary, who begged his forgiveness; she had just burned incriminating love letters and tried to burn the remaining powders. By the summer of 1751, it was too late for Francis, who died on 14 August; for Mary's dream of a relationship with Cranstoun, who escaped to Europe leaving Mary to face the consequences; and for Mary herself who was put under house arrest, given the suspicious circumstances. On one occasion, when allowed a walk outside the house, the locals proved hostile enough to chase her across the nearby bridge, so that she had to take refuge with a friend at a nearby inn.

After an inquest proved that Francis Blandy had indeed died from arsenic poisoning, Mary was committed to the Oxford county jail, and, while awaiting trial, she was made to wear leg irons to prevent her escaping. The case eventually came to court in March 1752. In spite of her story that the 'powders' were intended for a different purpose, her servants gave evidence against her, and her long-standing relationship with the adulterous Cranstoun did not impress the judge. The jury quickly decided her guilty of murder, which, of course, came with a death sentence.

Her last request, from the gallows, was distinctly middle class; for the sake of 'decency' she did not want to 'hang high' so that the men in the crowd could look up her skirts … a concern more for her modesty than for her death. The family home, Blandy House in Hart Street, Henley-on-Thames, now a dental practice, is said to be haunted by Mary's ghost.

BROWNRIGG, Elizabeth c.1720–67

Sadly, child abuse is nothing new, with Elizabeth Brownrigg, a midwife, one of its earlier known proponents. Elizabeth, a former servant, and her plumber husband, James, had become respected members of the community around Islington and the City of London.

Apprentices were supplied to her for £5 per head from 1765 when she was appointed overseer of the female inmates at St. Dunstan's workhouse. These apprentices were teenagers from the workhouse and they were the ones who suffered, rather than her own children – thirteen of whom survived infancy although only three made it to adulthood.

The experiences of Mary Mitchell, Mary Clifford and Mary Jones are detailed in the subsequent trial of Elizabeth Brownrigg. They were worked up to eighteen hours a day, clothed in rags, starved and beaten until bruised and bloody for the slightest infraction. It seems that Mary Jones escaped, seeking help at the London Foundling Hospital, but they took no action against the Brownriggs even though they made no attempt to explain her condition and ignored letters sent to them. To ensure she did not try the same thing, Mary Clifford was treated with even more severity, denied clothing, given the coal-hole for a bed, with a collar and chain round her neck to prevent her escape. Brownrigg used a horse-whip, a chain, a switch, or a bullwhip handle to inflict the regular beatings.

When neighbours began expressing concerns about the screaming they could hear from the Brownrigg household and a relative of Mary Clifford was denied access, the parish officials finally took notice and searched the house. They found Mary Clifford and Mary Mitchell with serious injuries and removed them to safety. However, it was too late for Mary Clifford, who died of her injuries a few days later.

Although Elizabeth's husband and grown son were also arrested and accused of wilful murder, all three having been found in hiding in South West London, the two men passed the blame on to Elizabeth. While they served six months Elizabeth received the death sentence, with early newspapers during the trial whipping up public resentment against her and her vicious behaviour. She was publicly hanged at Tyburn in front of a large, hostile crowd, her body dissected afterwards in the manner of the day; her skeleton was hung in Surgeons Hall. Why a caring midwife and loving mother felt the need for such violent treatment of her young helpers has been the subject of speculation ever since – more details of her crimes can be seen on the Newgate Calendar and Old Bailey websites.

BRYANT, Charlotte 1903–36

An illiterate Irish girl, Charlotte became promiscuous at an early age. However, she found her marriage (at nineteen) to a military policeman in the Dorset regiment serving in Derry did not help her escape the poverty trap because they promptly moved to a Dorset village where he took on lowly work as a farm labourer. Whether this move was due to her reputation as the local sex kitten in her home town, is not clear, but seems likely.

However, her husband, Fred, did not seem to mind her antics – which continued, repulsing the locals who knew her variously as Black Bess and Killarney Kate. Prostitution brought them in much needed extra money, especially with the five children she produced over thirteen years, not necessarily Fred's.

Fred did mind when Charlotte took one of her lovers in as a lodger on a regular basis from December 1933. This was gypsy Leonard Parsons, a horse trader, who was himself married. Even Fred's employer took umbrage and gave him his marching orders because of his wife's behaviour, so the couple moved to a different village – with Parsons still in tow.

It was May 1935 when Fred had his first bout of 'gastro-enteritis' followed by several others, each more agonising than the last, culminating in his death in December. But the post mortem found a much more unpleasant, and suspicious, cause of death; arsenic poisoning. Police found the burnt out remains of a tin containing arsenic-based weed-killer at the Bryant home and Charlotte was arrested and charged with murder in February, her children ending up in the workhouse. The general theory is that Charlotte wanted rid of Fred so that she could replace him with Parsons, unaware until late in the year that Parsons had a 'wife' or that Parsons may not have been willing to go along with Charlotte's plans.

At her trial in Dorchester in May, the defence lawyer asked the jury not to judge her promiscuity, only the evidence. Nevertheless, Parsons's sordid testimony with regard to their relationship did not do Charlotte any favours. So, ignoring her not guilty plea, the jury needed just one hour to find her guilty of murder, in spite of the lack of witnesses to her either buying the weed-killer or using it. Her execution was delayed for some weeks by a very vocal anti-capital-punishment campaign taking place outside Exeter prison. The execution took place behind closed doors, with several thousand people still demonstrating outside. She died protesting her innocence.

ELLIS, Ruth 1926–55

Ambitious from a young age to escape the poverty trap and find a better life for herself than her parents, who had moved from Wales to Hampshire during her childhood, Ruth's first attempt at a new life was at age eighteen. By 1944 she was expecting the baby of a Canadian serviceman but he turned out to be married with children – so she was not to be a war bride.

To support herself and her baby son she worked in a factory, a shop and restaurant and then found she could earn ten times as much as a hostess for a vice boss with a chain of Mayfair clubs – and brothels. In the hope of finding security, she married George Ellis, a dentist, in 1950, but his alcoholism and her jealousy meant she did not achieve her ambition. He committed suicide in 1958, but they had split up even before their daughter was born in 1951.

When they parted company, she had returned to her previous line of 'work' and took on two regular lovers. First was the glamorous racing driver David Blakely and then the older Desmond Cussen, both bored, and both, like Ruth, heavy drinkers.

While it would seem that the womanising Blakely was her favourite – in spite of their violent rows – he ended the relationship, with Ruth increasingly jealous about any new relationship she perceived. It seems that she was persuaded to take her revenge on him by Cussen, who gave her a loaded revolver to do the job. He drove her to Blakely's watering hole in Hampstead and Ruth, inebriated and oblivious, shot him at least four times as he ran from her. She then calmly asked a bystander to call the police.

Public interest was fuelled not only by this 'crime of passion' but by her blonde good looks, icy calm and straightforward confession. For some reason, she did not mention Cussen's involvement in court, though whether this would have made any difference is difficult to confirm. He, not so loyal at the end, denied all knowledge.

The Old Bailey jury took less than half an hour to decide her guilt. Aged just twenty-eight, Ruth Ellis was the last woman to be hanged in Britain – on 13 July 1955 at Holloway Prison. It does seem she was happy to die, believing it was deserved. A crowd of around 500 did not, however, agree, as they massed outside the prison gates for several hours calling for her reprieve – and there was a petition signed by thousands pleading for mercy because of the provocation of the violent Blakely. Albert Pierrepoint, the executioner, retired a few months later, having said that Ruth was the 'bravest of women'. It was this execution that added to the growing argument for the abolition of the death penalty. Ruth has certainly earned her place in history.

MAYBRICK, Florence 1862–1941

Although Florence was born in Alabama, she married James Maybrick, a much older (more than a twenty-year age gap) English cotton broker in London in 1881. She was from a comfortable, well-travelled, family, meeting him on a liner travelling between New York and Liverpool, a frequent journey for him, and the couple settled in Liverpool from 1884.

They lived in a grand mansion with five servants and had a son eight months after marrying and a baby girl in 1886. But, it transpired that James Maybrick had two weaknesses; women, and … arsenic. It seemed he believed that arsenic had aphrodisiac qualities – certainly his sexual demands were more than Florence could cope with. James, seemingly a bit of a hypochondriac, believed he had caught malaria and was convinced that a medicine based on arsenic helped him and that a tonic, also containing arsenic, was similarly beneficial.

In 1889, when Florence found out about his long-term mistress (and illegitimate children) she took his friend, Alfred Brierley, another cotton broker, to her bed, but received a black eye for her trouble.

Florence Maybrick, from Marshall & Cavendish Murder Casebook 1990.

By this time, James's drug-taking was becoming a real concern, with him gaining access to more supplies of arsenic via a 'clothier' who was experimenting with it in a cotton substitute. The marriage was becoming violent and James made a new will leaving most of his fortune to his children rather than his wife. In April 1889, Florence bought a large amount of arsenic-laden fly-papers which she later claimed she was going to use for cosmetic purposes, extracting the poison to improve her complexion – a not unknown theory. In May, James died, the post mortem discovering plenty of arsenic in his system and the inquest resulting in Florence's arrest and charge with her husband's murder.

A sign of the times was the public perception of Florence – once it was revealed that she had committed adultery, she lost credence. A letter she wrote to her lover, although their brief affair was over, was produced in court, with its reference to her husband being 'sick unto death' – interpreted as incriminating. The family nanny's evidence with regard to the rows between the couple did not help Florence's case.

The jury took only thirty-eight minutes to find her guilty, led by the judge who was obviously convinced of her guilt, regardless of the medical evidence that had been presented. She was sentenced to hang, but a hypocritical outcry from the press, who had vilified her as a murderous adulteress, resulted in the sentence being commuted to life imprisonment and she became a model prisoner for fifteen years, released in 1904.

But did she do it? She returned to the United States and gave talks about the need for universal penal reform, always claiming her innocence, and died in squalor in a tumbledown cabin in Connecticut. The truth? It died with her.

RATTENBURY, Alma 1897/8–1935

It was the 1935 murder of Alma's third husband, Francis Rattenbury, that led to her notoriety – and her death. Prior to that, she had been an accomplished musician in the country of her birth (Canada), married a Royal Welsh Fusilier who was killed in action, received the Croix de Guerre for her work with the French Red Cross and married Captain Thomas Pakenham after being cited in his divorce in 1921.

In a repeat performance, Alma was cited in Francis Rattenbury's divorce in 1925. She divorced Pakenham and married again the same year although Rattenbury was thirty years her senior. The couple fled scandal with Alma's son from her second marriage and moved to Bournemouth, where their own son was born. The birth finished the couple's love life seemingly due to Francis's impotence. He took to drinking, but Alma's song writing was achieving real success by now, until she was diagnosed with tuberculosis in 1932.

It was the hiring of eighteen-year-old George Stoner as chauffeur and handyman in 1934 that was the beginning of the end for Alma. A good-natured youngster, George was inexperienced and ready for seduction, though he apparently lied to Alma about his real age. She took him to London in 1935 for a five-day spending spree, showering him with gifts, paid for by her husband who thought he was paying for her to have a minor operation in the capital. On their return, Francis was not a happy man, and probably highly suspicious, so Alma planned for them to have a trip to Dorset to cheer him up but he was found with brutally-inflicted head injuries before this trip could take place.

Alma, hysterical, confessed to the attack, but it was George who was initially arrested because he had borrowed the wooden mallet used to bludgeon Francis. The attack proved fatal two days later and the decision was made to charge them individually with murder.

However, Alma withdrew her confession after her eldest son visited her and George, too, pleaded not guilty. She was acquitted and apparently turned down an offer of thousands for her story, but George Stoner was not so lucky, and was convicted. Public opinion was on George's side – the consensus was that he had been seduced and led astray by a much older woman, meaning that Alma was booed when she left the Old Bailey. Journalists followed her to a nursing home, this destination illustrating the effect that the trial, the grief, the shame and perhaps the guilt had on her. Days later, she stabbed herself six times, penetrating her heart. She left a note regretting only that she could not help George and he is said to have wept at her death. On appeal – supported by a petition containing 320,000 signatures! – he served just seven years of a life sentence, joining the Army on his release.

The murder and the trial caused quite a stir in Bournemouth. Souvenir hunters stole flowers from her grave and her garden. Was her suicide in vain in that George was not hanged anyway? Certainly the couple were more than just passingly fond of each other. Or was she in fact the guilty one?

SMITH, Madeleine 1835/6–1928

Madeleine's background was not the stereotype for a murderer. She was the eldest child in a rich Glasgow family and educated at 'Mrs Gorton's Academy for young Ladies,' a London boarding school. The family had a country residence on the Clyde as well as a city home with a number of servants. Typically Victorian, Madeleine's hobbies included creating seaweed pictures and making feather flowers.

MISS MADELEINE HAMILTON SMITH.—(FROM A SKETCH TAKEN DURING THE TRIAL.

Madeleine Smith, clipping from unknown 19th century newspaper.

Enter the personable, romantic and vain Emile L'Angelier, an older man employed as a lowly packing clerk but attracted by the idea of marrying into a prosperous family. They were introduced and became engaged but Madeleine's father refused his consent to the marriage. This did not deter her from succumbing to the Frenchman's advances in the spring of 1856, while realising it was (at the time!) 'very bad' – her feelings poured into letters delivered secretly by a friendly intermediary. They continued to meet, Madeleine growing more and more wary, especially when Emile threatened to show the letters to her father. It seems she asked him to burn them, but he ignored this request.

When she received a proposal from a better financial prospect in January 1857 she decided to accept, realising Emile's 'unsuitability' as a husband, but he refused to give her up without a fight – or to return her letters in spite of her pleas. Madeleine, due to marry in June, bought arsenic on several occasions in March (variously to kill rats or use on her skin …). Emile consumed coffee and chocolates provided by Madeleine during secret meetings, and died on the 23rd of that month. When her letters were discovered, his body was exhumed and hey presto … there was the arsenic. She was promptly arrested.

The trial made much of the hundreds of passionate letters penned by Madeleine, with at least sixty produced in 'evidence.' They were described as revealing evidence of 'disgrace … sin … [and] degradation'. She was described as 'a common prostitute' – with her deception of her father equally sensationalised. However, she had a strong defence lawyer who could show there was no evidence of her administering poison, or of a convincing motive. Additionally, he presented Emile as a 'vile seducer' who had corrupted an innocent girl and as a proven 'arsenic eater'. The jury decided that the unemotional Madeleine was not guilty, thanks to a majority verdict allowable in the Scottish courts.

In the meantime, her better prospect had faded from the scene, but she did marry, in 1861 – George Wardle, an artist. The marriage lasted until his death in 1885, after which she emigrated to the USA and was reported to have married again, this second husband dying in 1926, two years before her own death at ninety-three. It is fascinating to reflect on whether these two men knew about her background. As for Madeleine herself … Lucky? Probably. Innocent? Unlikely, surely. The debate continues.

THOMPSON, Edith 1893–1923

Edith, born in the East End of London, became an artistic, attractive teenager with impressive auburn locks. She turned quite a few heads, the most persistent – for six years – being Percy Thompson, a steady but unexciting shipping agent.

Her wedding day in 1916, overshadowed by war and Percy's imminent conscription, saw her having doubts. But the wedding went ahead, with Percy's active service short-lived because of a heart condition. It seems he may have deliberately fooled the army's medics.

She met Freddy Bywaters early in January 1920, a self-assured seventeen-year-old seaman, acquainted with her brothers. Percy foolishly assumed that Freddy was interested in Edith's sister, Avis and, even more foolishly, invited him on holiday with the three of them during the hot summer of 1921. Freddy then moved in as a paying guest and became deliberately land-locked, enabling him to spend more time with Edith. Finally, Percy became suspicious and the arguments started, driving Freddy from the house.

Now lovers, they went on meeting and Percy became more aggressive towards his wife. He could not stop her writing letters to Freddy, however, which eventually proved significant. With Freddy back at sea, the letters continued. She wrote of a failed attempt to poison Percy with quinine in his tea, suggesting she would try crushing glass in his food instead!

The tenor of the correspondence hereon suggested, however, that Freddy was cooling. But it seems that the physical intensity of their re-union after a particularly long spell apart diminished any mutual doubts they may have had. Their letters grew even lengthier, full of declarations of love.

Tuesday 3 October 1922 – the fateful day arrived. Edith and Percy were walking home after an evening at the theatre. Freddy was following them, until, close to home, he rushed out, stabbing Percy a number of times in the body and neck. As Edith went to Percy's aid, Freddy bolted. Neighbours who had heard screams appeared, with an ambulance called to what was now a dead body. Edith at this juncture seems to have been incoherent, suggesting Percy had had some kind of seizure.

Next day Edith was helping the police with their enquiries into what they regarded as murder. Freddy, too, was in custody. He seemed to come over as insolent in protesting his innocence, but it was simple for the police to find

The Trial of Edith Thompson. (*John Weedy*, Illustrated London News *1922*)

evidence against him – his bloodied clothes at his mother's home and the scores of letters he had kept from Edith for starters.

The press had a field day. Edith was decried as a wicked and debauched adulteress, the 'Messalina of Ilford', corrupting a mere boy and mistreating her inoffensive husband. At the trial, there were many references to passages in Edith's letters which could be interpreted as conspiracy to murder. Edith had also sent Freddy clippings of poisoning cases cut from newspapers, and admitted putting ground glass in her husband's tea, foiled when Percy complained of bitterness. Fantasy? Perhaps. Circumstantial evidence? Certainly. But, for a jury, convincing, with only two hours needed to find them both guilty.

Both appealed. A letter was published from Freddy's mother, broken-hearted at the prospect of losing her son. This led to the largest petition ever signed in Great Britain, Freddy seemingly having attracted more sympathy than Edith … but to no avail.

Freddy's hanging at Pentonville was less traumatic than Edith's at Holloway in January 1923. She was sedated, her hands and ankles tied and she had to be carried to the site. The hanging is recorded elsewhere in grim, repugnant detail, leading to the eventual suicide of the executioner and the retirement of the prison governor and chaplain. Her last words? 'I am not guilty.' So, if she knew nothing about Freddy's attack on Percy, which he maintained to the end was an impulsive drunken action, was she actually hanged for the immoral life she was perceived to have led?

TORRENCE, Helen ?-1752 & WALDIE, Jean ?-1752

Two women this time, with nothing known about their upbringing or childhood, but included partly because they committed a crime that is more often associated with men – murder in order to provide a dead body to the medical profession. Everyone has heard of Burke and Hare, a century later, but who knows about Torrence and Waldie?

What is known is that they lived a hand-to-mouth existence in the same Edinburgh tenement in the Royal Mile – Torrence was a seamstress, and Waldie a nurse. This was at a time when bodies were hard to come by for dissection and research and the women were attracted by the idea of earning an easy five shillings. Easy because Torrence knew of a sickly young boy, eight-year-old John Dallas, with a mother who liked a drink or two. The plan was to get the mother drunk, kidnap the tubercular boy (one of several children) and help him on his way with ale – although suffocation was seemingly what killed him in the end.

The two women had some problems hiding the corpse for the journey to the medical students, but the bulky Torrence managed to smuggle the body under her clothes, earning another sixpence for the 'delivery'. The body stayed under a bed until the time came for dissection, but no sooner had the students started 'work' than it became clear that Torrence and Waldie were under suspicion. The body had to be stitched back up in a hurry, and was disposed of unceremoniously – the students presumably having to return to the only other source of cadavers i.e. digging up fresh graves.

Suspicions had been fuelled by the boy's mother, by neighbours who had seen the two women in the area and by their suddenly having some spare cash. They were promptly arrested, each blaming the other for the murder but they were both found guilty and sentenced to be hanged. Torrence tried to claim pregnancy to escape execution but this was easily disproved. An interesting defence was also presented – they were 'only' guilty of kidnapping a live child and selling a dead child, neither of which were capital crimes!

Helen Torrence and Jean Waldie may well have started a sordid and macabre niche industry. Theirs were certainly the first known executions for what are known as anatomy murders. But were they just the first to be caught?

WARRISTON, Lady Jean 1579–1600

From a wealthy Stirlingshire family, Jean married the much older Laird of Warriston at a very young age (exact age unproven). If contemporary accounts are to be believed, the Laird treated his wife badly and she may well have been a victim of domestic abuse. On the other hand, there were also rumours about her relationship with a groom of her father's, Robert Weir. Just one of many questions that linger is; who was the father of her baby, born in wedlock?

Jean's nurse was very supportive, and apparently encouraged her to 'do' something about her abusive husband, and roped in Weir to 'help'. The three met up to discuss the situation and, the same night in July, Jean managed to ensure that her husband drank excessively. Weir hid in the cellar until she felt the time right to lead him to her husband, in his bed, although woken by their arrival. There is no doubt that Weir attacked the older man with some force, killing him, but it seems that he reassured Jean that he would take the blame if murder was the verdict, escaping by fleeing the country.

Next morning, the murder was, of course, discovered and Weir did indeed flee; but this left Jean and her servants to face arrest. So not quite the outcome they had planned. She is said to have found God and spirituality following her trial just a few days later, but had not displayed grief or remorse at the trial itself. Initially reluctant to confess, she was angered by religious intervention with local ministers putting her under pressure to confess; but, nevertheless, did finally admit to her involvement, although she tried unsuccessfully to exonerate her servants from blame.

Her wealthy father – or family – may have been influential in changing the manner of her death, although they felt dishonoured by her crime. Although she was sentenced to be strangled and then burned at the stake, this was changed to execution by the guillotine known as The Maiden, at an earlier time than usual to reduce the number of ghoulish witnesses.

After spending just two days in the Tolbooth gaol, Lady Jean faced her fate at around 3am on 5 July. She was able to give her baby son a final kiss and receive a forgiving kiss in her turn from her brother or brother-in-law (sources vary), although the family generally were in a hurry to get the event over with and to put the shame behind them. Regardless of the hour, plenty of people were there to watch her approach the scaffold, succumb to being blindfolded and calmly lay her neck on the block.

Her servants, including the nurse, did not have their sentences changed. They were strangled and burned at the stake in a different part of Edinburgh, with Weir finally arrested four years later and broken on the wheel; tied to a cartwheel on the scaffold and subjected to every bone being broken with a plough blade by the public executioner. Nasty.

Lady Jean, renowned for her beauty, had the kind of brief, dramatic life that has lived on in ballads. Blame within these verses is directed either at her, at her husband deserving of death, or the devil:

> *But Warriston was sair to blame,*
> *For slighting o' his lady so;*
> *He had the wyte o' his ain death,*
> *And his bonny lady's overthrow …*

WEBSTER, Kate 1849–79

Born into a poor Irish family, Kate moved to Liverpool as a teenager, having stolen the money for the ferry and served a four-year prison sentence for theft from the age of eighteen. This was the start of a criminal career.

Moving to London when released, she began to work as a cleaner. She didn't work for one family but moved around, sometimes as a cook or housekeeper and gave birth to an illegitimate son in 1874. The additional expense of a son prompted her to return to her previous life of crime and she served several prison sentences, leaving her son on those occasions with a friend who was also a domestic.

Julia Thomas, the woman she worked for in Richmond from January 1879 was not happy with Kate's work or her too-frequent visits to the local pub and she gave her employee notice. Kate pleaded for an extra few days' grace as she had no job and nowhere to live, granted by Mrs Thomas who seemed to be rather frightened of her at this stage.

After an evening service at church on Sunday 2 March, Mrs Thomas went home, where Kate was waiting for her; it seems an argument ensued, ending with Kate pushing her employer down the stairs to her death. Later forensic evidence suggests that she was killed with an axe before being pushed, not something that could be explained away.

The axe figures in the next grim episode. The body was dismembered and the body parts, with the organs either boiled or burned, packed into a wooden box – but with no room for the head or one foot which were put into a black bag. Kate then cleaned up the cottage, disposed of the remains,

Trial. Sentence & Execution of
KATE WEBSTER
For the Murder of Mrs. Thomas, at Richmond.

Behold a wretched woman dying,
Condemned to death for murder, see,
Kate Webster now in anguish crying,
'Twill end the famed Barnes mystery.
The Jury they have found her guilty,
Mrs. Thomas, you from there on high,
Behold your murderess now lamenting,
You'll be revenged—she's condemned
to die.

'Tis done, and I my death am waiting,
Kate Webster cries, why was I born,
To hear each witness against me stating,
For me it fills each heart with scorn
As link by link they were unfolding,
My fearful death I shall be beholding,
And meet a doom of infamy.

Can ere a wretch ere hope for mercy,
Was ever woman so vile as me,
I hope that God above will pardon,
And forgive when I'm in eternity.
Take warning by a wretched creature,
Who now in sorrow her death does wait,
While tears are streaming down every
feature,
No one will pity my awful fate.

I thought I ne'er should be discovered,
That fearful crime I could conceal,
But when the box it was discovered,
My mistresses murder it did reveal,
When captured how my heart was sinking,
That boy Porter the truth did say,
From guilt and death I now am shrinking,
In a murderer's grave I must lay.

Farewell to all, my child, my father,
For me the solemn bell will toll,
Oh, would a child I had died rather,
May God have mercy on my soul.
Oh, mistress dear, while you in heaven.
Your pity pray and pardon give,
And may I hope to be forgiven,
When on earth I no longer live.

Wandsworth Gaol,
Tuesday, July 29th, 1879.

This morning as soon as daylight set in, a body of people assembled in the vicinity of the Gaol, under the impression that something might be seen of the prisoner, but the execution was carried out within the prison walls. The gallows was erected in the large yard of the prison, a few feet from the ground. The only persons present were the Governor, Chaplain, the Sheriff, Marwood the Executioner, the representatives of the press, and a few gentlemen who had been granted the privilege to be present. When the bell of the prison began to toll, the prisoner appeared to feel the awful position she was in. On arriving at the scaffold, she turned round and thanked the officials for their attention to her during her confinement. She was then placed in the necessary position. The executioner having drawn the cap over her face, retired from the scaffold, and the signal having been given, the bolt was withdrawn, and the unhappy criminal was launched into eternity. A black flag was hoisted outside the gaol to denote that the execution had taken place.

On Sunday, April 13th, a black bag, sunk with two bricks, was taken out of the Thames below London-bridge. It was conveyed to the police-station and examined, as it was conjectured it might be the one which had contained the missing remains of the mutilated body, which through decomposition might have floated out.

On the boy however, being sent for to see if he could indentify it, he said it was not the same bag he carried. The bag is kept in the possession of the police, as it is considered possible that even perhaps a second bag might have been thrown in the water.

Old Bailey. 1879.

On Wednesday, July the 2nd, at the Central Criminal Court, before Justice Denman and a common jury, Kate Webster was placed in the dock on the charge of having on March 2nd, last, wilfully killed and murdered Julia Martha Thomas, at Richmond, in Surrey. The prosecution was conducted by the Solicitor-General, with whom were Mr. Poland, and Mr. A. L. Smith, and the prisoner was defended by Mr. Warner Sleigh and Mr. Keith Frith; Mr. J. B. Brindly watched the case on behalf of the witness Church.

The prisoner was quite pale. She wore a black cloth jacket, which was thrown open at the top, disclosing a small white knitted shawl. Her hair neatly and carefully arranged. During the reading of the indictment, she stood at the bar, but afterwards, at the suggestion of the learned judge, a chair was handed to her, and she sat down during the remainder of the hearing each day.

The Solicitor in stating the case for the prosecution, said the prisoner Webster, some time in the month of January or February, entered the service of Mrs. Thomas, the deceased, as general servant, leaving her son, a boy of five years of age, with a Mrs. Cressey, at Mitchell's-row, Hammersmith, with whom she had been living. Nothing more occurred to attract attention to the female prisoner until early in March, when the neighbours began to miss Mrs. Thomas, who had not been seen for some time. On March 4th, Webster went with a black bag to the house of a man named Porter, who lived a few doors from a quiet little beershop, and asked him to assist her in carrying it. As he should show, Porter and his young son then went with her to a beer-house in the Hammersmith Bridge-road. There Webster left them to go over the bridge, saying that she wanted to meet a friend. In a quarter of an hour she returned without the bag. She asked Porter to allow his son to go

with her to Richmond, and he consented, on condition that she sent him back the same night by the last train. The boy accompanied her to Mrs. Thomas's house. Presently Webster brought a deal bonnet-box of foreign make. The prisoner asked him to assist her in carrying it over Richmond Bridge, which he did. On the bridge she asked him to leave her for a moment, as she expected to meet a friend, and she would rejoin him shortly. The boy left her, but the night being dark he did not go far, and before he had got a few yards he heard a splash in the water. Just at the moment a tall gentleman was said to have passed over the bridge; but at present the police have no clue to the person, although it is possible they might hear something about him on a future occasion. A few minutes after the splash, Webster rejoined the boy, and told him that as it was then so late, half-past eleven—she should not send him home that night. Accordingly, he went to sleep at 2, Vine-cottages. Owing to the publicity given by the press, the facts ultimately became known.

On March 18th, two men went to the house of the deceased with a van for the purpose of purchasing the goods, but one of the neighbours—Miss Ives, seeing that the property was about to be removed, stepped out and made inquiries, which seemed to have put a stop to the proceedings, the men with the empty van went away. It also seems that Webster afterwards left the house, and was seen no more until she was brought back from Ireland. The same night she fetched her little boy and a black bag, and was driven in a cab to Hammersmith station, where she took a ticket for King's-cross, from there she went to Ireland.

The statement of Mr. Church is that he was at the Rising Sun on Monday evening, March 3rd, and that on Tuesday, the 4th, he was at the Kensington Licensing Sessions for the purpose of obtaining a renewal of his beer and wine license. After that he was at Sandown Races, and reached home from the races between six and seven

in the evening, and did not again leave his house. Webster stated that the crime was committed on March the 3rd.

Church says he never saw the woman until he was introduced to her to buy the furniture.

The elder Porter is very emphatic in his denial of Webster's allegations. In her confession the woman states that she had known the man for six years; but Porter points out that this is scarcely consistent with the fact that, when he took her to negotiate about the purchase of the furniture, he states he had no knowledge and was entire ignorance of that, and did not accept her assertion that they had known each other for the period mentioned. Another important statement by Webster is contradicted by Porter's son. The woman avers that on the night the box was thrown into the river, she met by arrangement, leaving the lad in the Road to wait. Young Porter now denies this.

On the sixth day of the trial, the jury retired at a quarter-past 5 to consider their verdict, and returned into court at twenty six minutes past 6 o'clock.

Mr. Avory, the Clerk of Arraigns, said, Gentlemen of the Jury, have you agreed upon your verdict?

The Foreman: We have

Mr. Avory: Do you find the prisoner, Catherine Webster, Guilty or Not Guilty of the murder of Julia Martha Thomas?

The Foreman: We find her GUILTY.

Mr. Avory: You say she is Guilty, and that is the verdict of you all?

The Foreman: Yes.

The prisoner then expressed her regret for implicating Church and Porter, and stated that the crime had been instigated by someone who had been her ruin. Sentence of death having been passed, the prisoner pleaded that her execution should be respited and began to live as 'Mrs Thomas' wearing the dead woman's clothes and claiming she had inherited the house.

In the meantime, the box of body parts had been found in the river and the foot on a manure heap but not identified as the head was missing, the case becoming known as the Barnes Mystery. Kate's behaviour now began to arouse suspicion – a young lad who had helped her carry the box to the river came forward and a neighbour started asking questions when some of the furniture and clothes were removed from the house and sold by Kate. They went to the police who searched the property and found the axe, together with charred bones and a handle that had come from the box in the river.

Days later, on 26 March, Kate was arrested – in Ireland, where she had predictably fled with her son. Back in Richmond, she was charged with murder but tried to blame the man who had bought Mrs Thomas's furniture – to no avail. She was transferred to Newgate prison, her trial at the Old Bailey set for 2 July.

Kate did not present a sympathetic figure in court. She had a tall, broad, masculine figure and features and showed no remorse. Thus, although the trial lasted several days, the jury took only an hour to find Kate guilty and although she claimed she was pregnant to escape execution this was easy to disprove.

She went down in history as the only woman hanged at Wandsworth Prison, in an execution shed known as the Cold Meat Shed, away from the public gaze – although it seems that a couple of newspaper reporters were in attendance. The vile nature of the crime meant that a model of Kate had appeared in Madame Tussaud's even before she had been sentenced! Her body was buried in an unmarked grave in an exercise yard in the prison.

Chapter Five

Gangsters, Thieves and Con-Artists

BLUFFSTEIN, Sophie c.1854–91

Known as the 'golden hand' because of her ability to swindle even the most sophisticated of punters, Sophie was apparently an attractive Russian brunette who married a small time banker who didn't meet her grand financial expectations. She left him to travel around Europe, coming up with a variety of frauds and scams to produce an income.

Her favourite swindle was to present herself as a well-heeled lady at an up-market jewellers and order expensive items to be delivered to the suite she had secured in a swanky hotel. As was the trusting custom of the time, the jewellers would arrange for payment to be collected after Sophie had taken delivery of the goods, but she had fled in the meantime, in each case leaving the hotel and, especially, the jeweller seriously out of pocket. She is rumoured to have been 'earning' as much as a quarter of a million pounds in just one year, and was able to live a lifestyle driving a carriage and pair around the cities of London, Vienna and Paris, where she was wanted by the various police forces.

When she was finally caught during another attempt to steal jewellery in Smolensk, Russia, she seduced the prison governor who freed her – and who left his wife and children to accompany her! Her freedom lasted until she attended a party which was raided by police looking for terrorists; finding Sophie Bluffstein was a bonus for them. She was sent to a notorious prison in Siberia, the Alexandrovsk, and kept handcuffed for two years of her imprisonment.

One author, Charles Hawes, who wrote about prisons in Siberia in 1904, also refers to her murdering a merchant, burying his body and making off with the thousands of pounds he was carrying, but there is no indication of an extra sentence in this regard. He does refer to her as being 'wan and thin from long confinement' and she would have had a hard time in Siberia.

Convicts were said to arrive on the island-based penal colony in iron cages on steamers and were hosed down with boiling water if they tried to attack their keepers, like wild animals. Many were kept manacled for longer periods than Sophie. The inmates were mainly murderers and the prison was regarded as a dumping ground for the worst Russian criminals who would be shot down if they were regarded as a threat.

Eventually, upon her release, she made a success of a hotel in Vladivostok, although this was towards the end of her life. Surely the most hardy and resilient of the women in these chapters.

BOCK, Amy 1859–1943

Amy, born in Hobart, Tasmania, had a mother who thought she was Lady Macbeth (and who died in an asylum in 1875), and a father with a penchant for amateur dramatics. No wonder that she developed an interest in acting and in dressing up, which came in very useful for her later role as con artist.

The family moved to Australia and Amy was well educated, gaining a position as a teacher, but soon in trouble for acquiring goods on false credit. Her father persuaded her to move to Auckland, where he was living with his second wife, and Amy took on a position as governess – but not for long, as she was soon in court for defrauding her employer but released because of her tearful confession and expressions of deep regret. This is where the acting came in and which was to be repeated on numerous occasions.

Amy worked her way around New Zealand as cook, housekeeper, governess or companion, her initially enthusiastic employers believing her intricate stories and giving her the opportunity to obtain false credit, to forge a cheque, or even pawn some of their furniture. Her first sentence was one month's hard labour for buying goods on false credit (1886), her second was six months' detention (1887) again for fraud. The detention centre was an 'industrial school' where the superintendent, impressed with her intelligence and her ladylike manners, also fell for her convincing stories and offered her a job as a teacher! But the offer was withdrawn when soon afterwards forged letters from a fictitious aunt attempting to engineer her release came to light.

A brief spell as a music teacher resulted in a two month prison sentence, again for false credit and another post as a governess resulted in a six-month sentence for larceny, with a housekeeper's job ending in three years' imprisonment with hard labour for pawning her employer's furniture. Seems no-one took up references in those days … or Amy forged them.

She joined the Salvation Army on her release but served another six months for stealing her landlady's watch, and was in prison over and over again for the next few years, now using a variety of aliases to cover her tracks and growing reputation.

Her most famous deception, but not her last, was posing as a wealthy sheep-farmer, Percival Redwood and wooing 'his' landlady's daughter, maintaining an impression of wealth with a host of small loans, which were not discovered until after their wedding! 'He' was arrested four days later and imprisoned yet again from 1909–1911. This was one occasion when the press really had a field day.

She did seem to stay out of trouble for a couple of years upon her release and married a farmer in 1914 but the marriage did not last because of the continuation of Amy's old tricks like stealing tennis club funds and not paying back her debts. The small-time frauds and petty thefts continued but slowly diminished, her final sentence being in 1931 when she was seventy-two – two years probation. Described then by a court reporter as a 'faded old lady' she finally disappeared from the radar.

CARABOO, Princess (aka Mary Baker) 1791–1864

Cobbler's daughter Mary Baker (nee Wilcocks) from Devon certainly knew how to attract attention. Not content with her life as a servant girl from a poor family, in and out of the workhouse, and losing an illegitimate child, she re-invented herself as an exotic 'foreign' princess. As Princess Caraboo, she begged her way to Almondsbury, Gloucestershire in 1817 where no one could understand the language she spoke; unsurprisingly, as it was her own invention. The local magistrate's wife took pity on this strange turbanned specimen and gave her a temporary home, fascinated by her behaviour – she slept on the floor, although with access to the luxuries of a mansion, and she avoided alcohol and meat, swam naked and prayed to Allah. According to the

Oxford Dictionary of National Biography, however, the less gullible husband had her locked up for vagrancy.

Interestingly, this is where she may have met a Portuguese sailor – one of several bi-lingual speakers who had been called upon to help with translation – who claimed to recognise the language and to 'translate' her story as that of a princess from the island of Javasu (?), who had been captured by pirates but jumped overboard in the Bristol Channel. What benefit he gained from this fabrication is not known; a share in her growing celebrity perhaps. It was her growing fame that was her undoing because she was apparently identified from her photograph – either in the *Bristol Journal* or the *Bath Chronicle* – by a landlady she had lodged with en route. The press then clamoured to reveal some of the stories at the expense of those this barely literate young woman had duped.

Mary Baker.

It seems that the truth may have been that Mary had married a man called Baker, familiar with travelling the Orient, who had deserted her. She had devised her new role while working in a bar and a brothel. No longer sympathetic, Mary's hosts quickly found her a passage on a ship bound for Philadelphia. Some accounts state that Mary was chaperoned on board, others that she was accompanied by her new friend, the Portuguese sailor, with £10,000 in goods and jewellery that had been bestowed on her by merchants who had mistakenly thought she qualified as a rich patron. She attempted to continue her role as a Princess in the USA, with less success and returned to Britain sometime between 1821 and 1824.

Although she married, and had a daughter, Mary still needed to make a respectable living once everyone had tired of hearing her adventures. She ended up selling leeches to the infirmary in Bristol, earning herself an above average income over many years. Her obituary in the *Bath Chronicle* of 19 January 1865 refers to her as having sustained a clever romance, but with her final trade a credit to herself and customers. They also refer to her daughter as being similarly 'possessed of considerable personal attractions'.

Postscript: there was also a story that she met Napoleon while on her travels (in St. Helena) and that he proposed to her … while fascinating, this is surely just that – 'a story'.

CARLETON, Mary (aka the German Princess) 1635 or 1642–73

Mary's early life lies shrouded in mystery, i.e. with regard to her birth and her family, but it is certain that she was well educated and brought up in Kent. Following her marriage to a Canterbury shoemaker, she had two children, both of whom probably died at a young age, leaving her free to 'escape' – to Barbados. Although her husband was instrumental in her return, she ignored him and bigamously married a rich Dover surgeon, claiming that she thought her first husband was dead, which let her off the hook.

Having a flair for languages, she escaped again – to Germany. There she took an older lover who showered her with expensive gifts and promised her marriage, until she left him – but not his gifts – at the altar. In 1663, she is recorded as being back in the U.K., posing as an orphaned German princess and extracting cash from the customers of The Exchange, a Billingsgate tavern, another skill for which she had a flair. Her apparent wealth attracted the inn-keeper's young brother-in-law, John Carleton, resulting in another bigamous marriage for Mary the same year. Some sources claim that this was not her third, but her fourth marriage.

This time, the authorities were informed (obviously not by a well-wisher) and she was tried at the Old Bailey for polygamy. Due to lack of evidence, she was acquitted. What she did next was audacious self-publicity – she wrote a (virtually) autobiographical play, *The German Princess*, and played the role for a theatrical group, viewed by even such luminaries as Samuel Pepys. Men seemed to find this persona irresistible, showering her with cash and jewellery.

For the next decade she duped gullible men and landlords – taking their silks, their silver, whatever she could lay her hands on. She got away with it because most were too embarrassed to admit how they had been deceived, but

The German Princess *with her suppos'd* Husband *and* Lawyer.

THE *German* Princess was so called from her pretending to be the Daughter of *Henry Van Wolway*, Doctor of the Civil Law, and Lord of *Holmstein* in *Germany*. But she was really the Daughter of one *Meders* a Chorister of *Canterbury* Cathedral in which City she was Born the 11th of *January*, 1642. Her first Husband was one *Stedman*, a Journeyman Shoemaker: from whom eloping, she married a Surgeon at *Dover*. This being discovered, she was Try'd at *Maidstone* for Polygamy. But getting Acquitted she ventured on a third Marriage to one *Carleton* a Londoner, whose Name she usually bore when she was pleased to put off the Princess. Her Tricks were innumerable both in *England* and *Germany*; for tho' she was not a Native of the latter Country, as she pretended, yet she went thither, and made a Property of many Gallants at the *Spaw*, a Place like the *Bath* in *England*. Her principal Talent lay in deceiving People, with the pretence of having a large Fortune; For by this Means she got Presents from Suitors, and Credit from Tradesmen; whom she always left in the Lurch. Being at last Apprehended for stealing a silver Tankard, she received Sentence of Death; but got it changed for Transportation: However she ventured to come Home, and set up once more for an Heiress. By this Means she married an Apothecary at *Westminster*, whom she robbed of 300l. and then left him. She was detected in *Southwark*, by the Keeper of the *Marshalsea* Prison; being carried to the *Old-Bailey*, she confessed who she was, and received Sentence of Death a second Time. She Suffered with a great deal of Resolution and seeming Penitence, on the 22d. of *January*, *Anno* 1674. in the 38th. Year of her Age. The Lawyer represented in the Plate was one that she applied to under Pretence of Business, and from whom she extorted 100l. by the help of a sham Husband, who pretended to be Jealous of catching them together.

Mary Carleton with her supposed husband.

even when she did appear in court her silver tongue meant that she managed to avoid jail. Amazingly, even when transported to Jamaica in 1671 following her theft of a silver tankard, she managed to find her way back again to this country just two years later. Posing as a rich heiress, she seems to have married (again) a wealthy apothecary, leaving him almost penniless soon after!

Whether it was this man or another who finally brought her again to court is not known. She was tried for a string of crimes, including her return from transportation without permission. The result hardly needs documenting; execution by hanging, but, even at the end, Mary dressed at the height of fashion for her last moments at Tyburn, a picture of John Carleton attached to her sleeve.

DIAMOND, Alice 1884–1962

Diamond Annie, as she became known, was born in Lambeth Workhouse in South London to a family of criminals, and had a criminal record – for theft – by the age of seventeen. The area she lived in was known for its gangs of lawless thugs and thieves, gangs that had been roaming the streets for decades. During the First World War, she was arrested for using another girl's identity card to gain entry to an ammunition factory where it is assumed she was trying to steal explosives to use in blowing up safes.

The Elephant Gang (from the Elephant and Castle area) was probably the worst, with a history of cut-throats dating back to the days of the highwayman. After the First World War they needed a leader for their army of female shoplifters, the Forty Elephants (or Forty Thieves) – a role that could earn real respect. Enter Alice – or Annie. She became the mastermind behind large scale and systematic shoplifting in the department stores of London's West End, or pickpocketing those queueing for the theatre. The clothes the girls wore were specially made with capacious 'knickers' known as hoisting drawers, and large hidden pockets to aid their transactions and Annie ensured they had access to a chain of fences. They were known to arrive in groups in taxis or limousines, and see off any women trying to work their patch – with ferocious violence if necessary.

The girls had their own dress code when not working – they did not wear stolen clothes because they could afford to buy high fashion, and apparently were quite a glamorous bunch; their men were, unsurprisingly, notorious gangsters. Because of the way they looked, some of the girls were also adept at 'getting to know' aristocrats with guilty secrets and earning a good living by blackmailing them, a nice little sideline. Some were also said to have found jobs in luxury mansions where they were in the ideal position to plan burglaries.

Annie was quite tall, around 5ft 8in, and could handle herself in a fist fight, which saw her in trouble a few times for affray as well as for theft. She was also said to be useful with a steel blackjack (a form of cosh) and her famous diamond rings served as a useful knuckleduster. All her girls were arrested regularly, but they had plenty of funds to pay bail money.

Some of Annie's jail sentences involved hard labour, but she was not deterred and carried on until at least 1929. This seems to have been her last conviction – but not necessarily her last offence.

Postscript: Annie's successor, Shirley Pitts, had an even longer career in crime, some fifty years, and was apparently buried in a £5,000 Zandra Rhodes dress she 'forgot' to pay for!

FERRERS, Catherine 1634–60

A controversial entry, perhaps, but a fascinating character that deserves inclusion. Controversial because of the doubts attached to her 'story' … that of a female highwayman terrorising Hertfordshire during the English Civil War before dying of gunshot wounds sustained during a robbery.

Catherine has been re-named 'The Wicked Lady' in history, and on film. Historians have proved that she existed and was from an aristocratic family, with a substantial inheritance. Orphaned at a young age, she became a ward of the Fanshawe family and was married to the dissolute Thomas Fanshawe aged just thirteen, solving the Fanshawe's financial problems temporarily until the money ran out. Cromwell's army and civil unrest were also impacting on her comfortable existence.

It is unlikely that Catherine would have embarked upon a criminal existence for money, rather out of boredom with her husband spending too much time in the Tower of London for his political views. What has not been proved is the idea of her leading a double life as noblewoman and highwayman, with facts being hard to come by. For instance, she is said to have been taught her unlawful skills by highwayman Ralph Chaplin, but even Ralph's very existence has proved elusive. But she has a reputation for operating alone (perhaps after his death?), becoming more brutal and ruthless, even killing a parish constable. Arson, stealing cattle, robbery, it was all apparently considered quite an adventure until she shot and killed a wagoner, oblivious to the men hidden by straw bales in the wagon – one of whom returned fire, wounding her fatally.

She died a few days later and was buried at St. Mary's, Ware, but if it is true that the burial was carried out hastily, in secret, at night, outside the Fanshawe vault, then the question of why this was necessary comes into play – unless it was necessary to hide the manner of her dying and the scandal that would bring. There are other candidates for the origins of The Wicked Lady stories, but Catherine seems the most likely. No smoke without fire springs to mind.

FRITH, Mary (known as Moll Cutpurse) c.1584–1659

Born to a shoemaker in London's Barbican, Mary was in trouble with the law from the age of sixteen, her first indictment for theft (of 2s 11d). Although her uncle, a minister, tried to send her to New England for a new start, she jumped ship and continued her wild life as what was known as a 'roaring girl'. This involved sometimes dressing as a man, complete with sword, drinking and smoking (perhaps the first woman to smoke in England) and expertly cutting the strings of the leather purses of as many as fifty victims per day. This form of theft is one of the reasons attributed to her nickname, but another is the fact that she cut purses from leather for a living before taking up petty crime.

Mary also earned money as a fortune-teller and befriended members of the Society of Divers ('diver' being slang for pickpocket). She is recorded as having been burnt in the hand at least four times, a common punishment for thieves and having served prison sentences in Bridewell prison. As for her habit of wearing men's clothing, this had two outcomes; one was being asked to perform on stage at the Fortune Theatre in around 1611, making a mockery of the law against dressing as a man. She entertained the audience with her defiance and oddity – and lute-playing. Secondly, this challenge to convention that may have resulted in her being sentenced for dressing indecently in an attempt to discourage others. She did public penance in a white sheet during morning sermon at St. Paul's Cross, probably in 1612, this punishment for cross-dressing having little effect on her exhibitionism and defiance, but with no further repercussions.

In March 1614, this masculine and homely female married a mystery figure named Lewknor Markham who promptly disappears from her story (the marriage may have been merely to establish some form of respectability). A few years later, she moved on to fencing goods rather than stealing them. She is also said to have become a pimp, procuring either women or men, depending on the need. More famously, she rode from Charing Cross to Shoreditch in London on a famous performing horse named Morocco; she was dressed as a man, with a banner and trumpet providing plenty of razzmatazz and earning her £20 as the result of a bet. Her lifestyle was certainly profitable as she is said to have had three maids at her Fleet Street home; she also kept pampered dogs and other pets.

Even when approaching sixty, Mary was still outrageous because this was when she joined her highwayman friend, Captain James Hind, in robbing Parliamentarians during the Civil War. General Fairfax was apparently her most famous victim – she is alleged to have shot him, robbed him of 250 jacobuses (gold coins) and killed two of his horses to prevent pursuit. For this she was captured, tried and sentenced to death, but managed to arrange a meeting with General Fairfax and offered him £2,000 (a considerable amount of money) to procure her pardon – the truth may well be more complicated. She was reprieved, though, and ended up in Bethlem until being 'cured' of insanity and released in 1644 to run the Globe tavern in Fleet Street.

With freedom, however, came the onset of dropsy, an unpleasant contemporary complaint, which ended her life in 1659. Her will asked that she be buried 'breech upwards' to be outrageous in death as in life. It seems her wish was granted (note that such a wish is disputed by the *Oxford Dictionary of National Biography* contributor, Paul Griffiths), and her remains lie in St. Bride's, Fleet Street, her lavish earnings almost spent.

GOLDSTEIN, Lilian 1902–76

Society beauty Lilian was the British equivalent of Bonnie Parker, though not as bloody, her partner-in-crime being Charles 'Ruby' Sparks. It is not known how the middle-class girl from Wembley, who was a skilled seamstress, met the jewel thief and serial convict Sparks, whose father was a fence. Perhaps their connection was via Harry Goldstein, whom she married in 1920, a man who seemed to have acted as her pimp and who had served three months hard labour for living off her immoral earnings. According to James Morton in *East End Gangland*, Harry was subsequently sentenced to eighteen months imprisonment for 'carnal knowledge' of an under-sixteen-year-old; this was after Lilian had become associated with Sparks.

Ruby got his name from one of his earliest burglaries when he stole a Maharajah's box (from his mansion or from a train, reports vary) and gave away the contents, thinking they were red stones when they were actually £45,000-worth of rubies. He was born around 1910 and by the mid-1920s was a serious and well-known criminal, who had specialised in raiding country houses until, apparently, he met Lilian who persuaded him to try throwing bricks through the windows of jewellery shops. Certainly she became known as the brains behind the duo.

As for Lilian, she was known to drive a big Mercedes and became known as the bobbed-haired bandit, becoming Ruby's getaway driver. She was easily recognisable especially when she wore her favoured red beret and matching coat! They were the first 'modern' robbers in Britain to use a car for their robberies. As an ex-seamstress, Lilian was useful to Ruby in stitching up his wounds, and used bulldog clips to hold his wounds together after a smash and grab until she had the opportunity to fix him up.

Their first arrest together seems to have been in 1927 in Manchester but Ruby protected her so that she escaped punishment – soon after, Lilian waited outside Strangeways for him during an escape attempt that went wrong so that she had to drive off without him. Ruby served a number of sentences, but acquired a reputation for escaping from most of the prisons where he was detained.

The couple were also arrested again in Blackpool in 1930 – in her case, for receiving – but the case against her was dropped. Ruby, however, was given another sentence; five years for robbery, with another escape attempt following. In 1939, while serving another five years, he escaped – from Dartmoor – and he and Lilian were both arrested again, she for 'comforting, harbouring, assisting and maintaining' Sparks. She broke down in court, saying she was afraid of him and that he had threatened to kill her. Although she was sentenced to six months, she only served three weeks of her sentence thanks to a sympathetic judge. Of their fourteen years 'together', he had spent twelve locked up, so not the most successful gangster in history.

After the Second World War, they both gave up their unlawful lives. Ruby married a respectable girl and opened a club in Regent Street, and Lilian decided she had had 'enough of this bandit lark' and faded into insignificance. But she lives on in police records because of the respect she had earned with regard to her outstanding, and effective, driving ability.

PARKER, Bonnie 1910–34

A short life that will long be remembered. Born in Texas, she was a bright and pretty student with ambitions to be an actress, but whose judgment of men as she grew up was poor. Days before her sixteenth birthday, while still at school, she married a classmate, Roy Thornton, and had his name tattooed on her right thigh. He was an abusive husband and sent to prison for robbery in 1929, ending their relationship, though they never officially divorced.

When she met Clyde Barrow a year later, he was already an ex-con although

Bonnie Parker.

only twenty and wanted by the police. The couple do appear to have developed a real and intense affection for each other, but he was soon caught, convicted of auto theft and returned to prison. Bonnie smuggled a gun inside for him and he escaped but, captured a week later, ended up with a sentence of fourteen years hard labour. It was his mother who managed to get him out on parole in 1932, meaning that he and Bonnie could be re-united.

This was the start of their crime spree, using stolen cars. The diminutive Bonnie was soon captured during a failed robbery attempt and sent to prison for two months but persuaded the courts that she had been kidnapped by the Barrow gang. Together again, the gang continued the robberies, killing several people along the way, including law enforcers. They operated over five states of America, giving law enforcement agencies a run for their money. They did not just target banks but also robbed gas stations and grocery stores with paltry takings.

Bonnie was debilitated to some extent because of a car accident in June 1933 when she was Clyde's passenger. The third degree burns from the battery acid left her with a limp – rather like Clyde, who was missing a big toe thanks to an earlier attempt to escape jail. They came close to capture the same year when their hideouts were raided, with Clyde's brother killed. But the couple evaded capture for another year, enough time to earn a reputation as outlaws, with posed photographs left behind (deliberately?) at the location of at least one shoot-out, delighting the press.

After the Texas murder of two highway patrol officers, followed by that of a constable in Oklahoma, the police forces closed in. Bonnie and Clyde drove into an ambush in Louisiana on 23 May 1934 and were killed in a hail of bullets. It is likely that the ambush was arranged by a father of one of the gang, Henry Methvin, to achieve leniency for his son. However, the finale was achieved, the news promptly brought souvenir-hunters who arrived to cut off locks of hair and pieces of clothing from the couple before the bodies were removed, such was their celebrity status. The newspapers were full of the Bonnie and Clyde story, publishing extra editions to mark the two funerals.

Bonnie never had the opportunity to make it as an actress, but there is more than one way to achieve fame …

FARRELL, Sadie c.1855–?

Fact or fiction? If Sadie had been a man, more evidence would no doubt be available, but she was born in an era which tended to ignore erratic female behaviour, attributing it in the main to female sensitivity or insanity. For the purposes of this book, she and her lifestyle are regarded as being fact.

With Irish roots, but born in a New York slum, it is not surprising perhaps that she grew up with muggers and hustlers, at a time of the famously violent Gangs of New York in the mid-nineteenth century. She worked the local docks, butting her victims in the stomach – hence her nickname, Sadie the Goat – with a male accomplice rendering the victim unconscious with a slingshot. Then he would be stripped of all his possessions, even his clothes.

The age-old English-Irish clash became significant for Sadie when she had a run-in with English-born 'Gallus Mag', a six-foot female bouncer who collected the ears she had bitten off! By upsetting Mag, Sadie's ear joined her collection. Sadie switched to the other side of town, meeting up with the inept Charlton Street Gang in around 1869, all brawn and no brains. She supplied the brains so that their attacks on merchant shipping achieved greater success. Initially operating out of row-boats, they moved on to a sloop under Sadie's guidance, displaying a Jolly Roger from the mast and moving their efforts to the more lucrative Hudson River. The gang did not steal just from shipping; they also robbed farm-houses and riverside mansions. Sadie was instrumental in finding plenty of fences that welcomed her 'contributions' including New York's Marm Mandelbaum, the powerful and notorious Queen of Fences who is said to have run a school for criminals.

Kidnapping (for ransom) and even murder were to be added to the gang's agenda, and there are stories of Sadie forcing those who gave her trouble to walk the plank, though whether this is true is less likely than other accounts of Sadie's activities. Hudson Valley residents eventually banded together and, with the help of an early harbour police patrol, ambushed the gang, apparently killed some of its members and left Sadie to return to her early haunts. But now she was known as the Queen of the Waterfront, with enough cash to open her own gin mill! Even Gallus Mag gave her back her ear, which she is said to have worn in a locket for the rest of her life – trouble is, no one seems to know how much longer that was.

Sadie is, however, referenced in a number of historical novels, and in a twenty-first century ballad. It is hard to believe that she did not exist, though no doubt there has been some embroidery over the years.

SERRES, Olivia 1772–1834

This is one fascinating woman who channelled her imagination in the wrong direction. Her parents moved to London after her father was found to have indulged in a sideline as an embezzler, so Olivia spent many formative years with her academic uncle. Although her father earned some income painting (he painted walls, not canvases) her talent initially was more artistic and, in 1791, she married her drawing master.

The couple separated in 1802, leaving Olivia with three young children, one of whom may not have been her husband's as she was known to have had several affairs. She supported herself by painting and teaching. Impressively, she actually obtained a post as landscape painter to the Prince of Wales (later George IV) in 1806. After exhibiting at the Royal Academy and the British Institution, however, her imagination began to run riot. She produced an opera, a novel and other literary works, but achieved fame as the author of controversial letters in the *Gentleman's Magazine*.

Escalating this fantasy world, Olivia now claimed that a whole host of 'evidence' proved that she was the daughter of George III's youngest brother. The seventy-plus documents produced even included a marriage certificate dated 1767 naming this duke and her uncle's sister as her parents. However, the Princess Olivia of Cumberland who turned up at high profile London dinner parties sporting a coach with royal arms did not convince anyone and nor did her documents, many written or witnessed by those who had since conveniently passed away. She was lucky not to have been prosecuted for forgery, especially as the likes of Sir Robert Peel refuted her claims on the floor of the house.

Not for the first time, Olivia was arrested for debt in 1821, the same year she was re-christened as Olive, her 'mother's' name, claiming exemption from proceedings because she was a member of the royal family. This didn't work and she served her time in the King's Bench prison in Southwark, but continuing to come up with fantasies – she also claimed to be a descendant of the King of Poland! Her estranged husband died in poverty in 1825, his will repudiating her claims. As for Olivia-Olive, who survived another decade of frequent imprisonment for debt, she also died 'in the rules of the king's bench'. Interestingly, her daughter inherited her mother's fantasising, assuming the title of the Duchess of Lancaster – but when she took the case to court to claim her legacy it was thrown out.

SHARPE, Mary (Chicago May) c.1876–1929

Born into a hard-working Irish farming family, it did not take May (her 'adopted' name) long to tire of her industrious but poor family and their smothering Catholicism. At just nineteen, she stole the family's life savings of around £60 and ran off to the USA leaving stories behind her of already seducing and blackmailing the son of a leading Irish family.

There are conflicting accounts of her relationships in the US including her first marriage, to James Sharpe. Did he secure her release from prison? Did he leave her a widow before her twenty-first birthday, or did they merely divorce? It seems to have been cattle rustler and safe-cracker Dal Churchill who passed on some of his 'skills' to May before her marriage. But Dal was apparently killed by vigilantes after a train robbery.

The facts of May's 'career' are on firmer ground. In Chicago, she learned the Badger Game; luring men to her hotel room, robbing them and then blackmailing them with the threat of telling their wives what they were up to. She was adept at this confidence trick, accumulating some £300,000 when still a teenager and becoming part of the local, violent, criminal fraternity. This provided a splendid home, bodyguard, servants and film star wardrobe.

Moving her operation to New York, it is said that she tried conning the author Mark Twain but he didn't fall for her stories. Although adept at pick-pocketing, she also tried her hand as a chorus girl in a Broadway musical, bearing in mind she was tall, striking and with unusual auburn hair. More lucrative was finding a corrupt police officer who seemingly supplied targets for the Badger Game, taking twenty-five per cent for his trouble.

Realising that what she had to offer was not limited to the US, May travelled around, testing the ground in places as far apart as Cairo and Rio de Janeiro. She settled in London for a time, becoming the mistress of Eddie

Guerin, an Irish ex-convict. She was his accomplice in a £250,000 robbery at American Express in Paris in 1901, but an informer meant that they did not benefit from the proceeds. She was convicted only of smuggling the proceeds back to London, although this did mean her serving four years hard labour in a Montpelier prison. Eddie got a life sentence, but managed to escape – from Devil's Island.

Upon her release, May tried re-visiting her childhood home but the community was even more judgmental than expected. She ended up in London setting up the Northumberland Avenue Gang, active as madam, blackmailer and with an opium den!

When Eddie escaped, it seems he arranged for her to be maimed, suspecting she had betrayed him. Charley Smith (an alias), the man sent to do the deed, however, ended up as her lover until Eddie was released in 1907 after another spell in prison. The two men confronted each other in London, resulting in Eddie being shot. May and Charley were charged with attempted murder, with one suggestion that it was May who primed Charley because of her fury at Eddie's relationship with a much younger woman. This time May was sentenced to fifteen years (Charley got life) and ordered out of Britain on her release around ten years later. The British newspapers gave her a hard time, claiming that her blackmailing was driving men to suicide.

Apparently returning to the USA in the 1920s she – in turn – was conned out of her remaining funds by a young, long-standing (but low life) lover she had come to trust. May was now reliant on small time theft for a small time income. An attempt to raise funds with her autobiography did not pay and she ended up as a street-walker, charging just a couple of dollars a time. She had also developed an alcohol habit.

While difficult to confirm the truth about her final days, it seems that Charley may have re-appeared in her life at this time – indeed, she may have died on their planned wedding day! The Queen of Crooks was described, at the end, by Reuter, as 'The Worst Woman in The World' … hmm.

STARR, Belle 1848–89

Belle (born Maybelle) was born into a wealthy family but her father, a slave-owner, and mother, were involved in a bloody feud with another Missouri family. This may have prompted Belle, as early as the age of ten, to have been reported riding around sporting two guns. The family inn gave her the opportunity to learn blackjack and faro – successfully.

Her education was, however, conventional. She showed a flair for languages and piano at the all-female academy she attended, but as a natural tomboy she was happier in the company of men. Bud, her

Statue of Belle Starr, sculpted by Wolfgang Sauber, in Woolaroc, Oklahoma.

hunting-shooting-fishing older brother, was an early influence, but they were separated when he joined the Southern Confederacy at the outbreak of Civil War. He became a captain after a stint as a bushwhacker, using his Native American skills. With his influence, Belle, too, was given a role, carrying intelligence, and delivering information on the Union troops. But Bud was killed in action and the family fled to Texas in 1864, much to Belle's dismay.

Their wealth gone, the family worked the land, with Belle earning extra money with faro dealing. Socially, they mixed with others who had similar resentments. These included Jesse James and his family, many of whom had been bushwhackers, too. Belle enjoyed their company and rode with them when she could. At eighteen, she had a relationship with Jim Reed, producing a daughter, but neither of them were ready for dutiful home life. When Jim was wanted for murder, in 1871, they ran off to California, and had a son.

Although they tried farming a small patch of land given to them by Belle's father, Jim was soon involved in a number of notorious robberies and he was gunned down in 1874 a few months after robbing a stagecoach. Belle's life began collapsing: her father died; her mother moved to Dallas with Belle's daughter; her son left home; and she moved on – to the notorious Starr family she had known before Jim Reed came along.

In 1880, she married Sam Starr, with a honeymoon allegedly spent rustling cattle. They lived in a cabin with an allotment provided by the Cherokee Nation in accord with his heritage. Jesse James hid out there at one point. The couple were arrested for horse-stealing in 1883, when she was said to be concealing a six gun and two pistols in her clothes. This led to her nickname of Queen of the Outlaws, although both were released from jail within the year. Now sporting a sombrero and velvet riding habit, Belle began to relish her rebellious reputation – apart from the attention it attracted from the local newspapers who reported her every move and printed photographs of her with convicted criminals.

Her husband, too, was targeted by local law officers who were convinced that he was involved in bootlegging, rustling and horse theft – a not inaccurate summation. In December 1886, when Belle was reunited with her children, Sam was in a shoot-out with a police officer who had been on his tail, both men dying as a result. Belle continued the life she knew without him, being arrested several times in the years that followed, but released due to lack of evidence.

She soon found a new lover, the much younger Cherokee Jim July, causing problems between her and her son, only seven years Jim's junior. She drove out her pregnant daughter, refusing her consent to the girl's marriage. Rows followed with Jim and with their tenant, a wanted man she could have been accused of harbouring. This man, Edgar Watson, was accused of her murder in February 1889. She had been shot twice while riding home, a few days before her forty-first birthday. There was not enough evidence against him, however, nor against her son whose motive could have been the whipping she gave him when he spoke out against Jim. Even Jim himself was under suspicion as the couple had been going through a rough patch. Plenty of fiction has been woven into Belle's story over the years, so it can be difficult retrieving the facts. One thing is certain – her reputation lives on.

TANN, Georgia 1891–1950

Thanks no doubt to the influence of her father, a Mississippi judge, Georgia's ambition was to become a lawyer in a male-dominated profession rather than a concert pianist in accord with his wishes. Although she studied music in Virginia she stood out with her limp – the result of a car accident – her big feet, masculine frame, her trousers and cropped hair.

At twenty-two, she moved on to do what she wanted, studying social work, specialising in the new field of adoption. She began matching lower class children with middle class parents, regarding the poor families as irresponsible and the richer families as morally sound. It was from this time that she appeared to enjoy effectively playing God. This was reinforced in 1922 when she stole two children from an impoverished and sick local woman, luring the boys into her car and arranging for her father to rule the mother an unfit parent.

Escaping local disapproval, she moved to Tennessee, becoming director of a Memphis children's orphanage, with a corrupt local mayor who turned a blind eye. This is where she started forging the birth certificates of these poor children to avoid concerns from early geneticists with regard to their 'bad blood'. The certificates would show higher status parents. She now had two secrets to keep – the forgeries, and her lesbian lifestyle, the latter at a time when lesbians were considered deviants.

Professionally, within a year, she was controlling the lives of every available – or unavailable come to that – adoptee in Tennessee. She became involved not just in state adoptions, but in private adoptions which commanded as much as $5,000 per child for Georgia. There were no controls over the motives of the adopters who could be paedophiles or couples looking for a workhorse – all they needed was the cash. Babies were sold in all parts of North and South America, and even as far as the U.K. Georgia also had Hollywood names among her clients – for instance, Joan Crawford, June Allyson and Lana Turner.

As demand began to exceed supply, Georgia started bribing nurses and doctors to give up babies as having been 'stillborn' – regarding the mothers simply as breeders for her profit. No doubt many of these babies did indeed die, following abuse at the hands of their adopters. She even recruited women to spot neglected or lone children that could be kidnapped from their gardens or schoolyards. There were reports of single mothers returning to the nursery to collect their child to be told that their child had been taken into care by welfare officers … The local family court judge was also taking a cut because she assisted Georgia's cause by sending hundreds of children to orphanages unnecessarily, leaving them vulnerable pawns in Georgia's 'business'.

The trafficking - for this is was it was – continued unabated until 1948, when a new state governor began investigating a trickle of complaints, finding that the paperwork surrounding these 'adoptions' was often destroyed. He found that children at the Memphis orphanage had been neglected, beaten and abused, with 'dysentery' being given as the cause of death of nearly fifty children in 1945.

But by now, Georgia had made a fortune and owned several properties and a hotel. She did not have much longer to enjoy her spoils, however, as in 1950 she was diagnosed with cancer before the governor's findings were announced. The official solution was to regard the 5,000 adoptions she had processed to be regarded as legal, erasing all those histories and leaving heartbreak behind her.

YOUNG, Mary (known as Jenny Diver) c.1704–41

It seems likely that Mary was born (illegitimately?) in Ireland, and she has been attributed with a variety of names, Jenny Diver being a popular name for a female pickpocket. She was almost certainly still a young teenager when she moved to London to learn her future trade, accompanied en route, some say, by a potential husband who had robbed his master and subsequently suffered the consequences – a death sentence. But she became what the Newgate Calendar regarded as 'one of the most artfullest Pick-pockets in the World' thanks to her introduction to a number of expert thieves, very much the artful dodgers of their day.

Jenny was not just your run-of-the-mill pickpocket or con artist – she introduced sophisticated innovations like false hands, concealing her real hands and their activity beneath voluminous clothing, sometimes faking pregnancy with a cushion. She once stole a purse from a well-wisher who was treating her with salts for a fainting fit (driving off afterwards in the poor woman's coach!), and similarly used members of her 'gang' to empty the pockets of onlookers when she faked a similar fit in busy Hyde Park.

Unlike some of her contemporaries, Jenny was not unattractive and would put this to good use, luring at least one rich young man as far as her lodgings, where he was compelled to hide, once undressed, because 'her husband' had returned. This gave the enterprising Jenny the opportunity to relieve him not just of his clothes but their contents which included a diamond ring and a gold-headed cane.

By this time, Jenny and her band of brigands were travelling between London and Bristol but she was finally arrested for theft and sentenced to deportation to the American colonies in 1733 after spending four months in Newgate prison. It appears that, having dealt in stolen goods while in prison, she was able to pay for a more comfortable berth on her convict ship. In America, it seems she persuaded another infatuated young man to pay her passage home, although whether she actually needed his financial help is debatable. Mary was lucky to get away with so much for so long – returning before a transportation term expired was a capital offence, added to the fact that on the day she arrived the first thing she did was to attempt to rob an old woman. But she continued to practice her profitable art, using a variety of pseudonyms, until another arrest for picking a gentleman's pocket, for which she was sentenced yet again in 1738 to transportation (as 'Jane Webb').

Back a year later, she had not changed her ways, although her gang had dispersed. She was inevitably re-arrested for stealing thirteen shillings, this time being given the death sentence as her aliases had failed to work. At her trial, some accounts claim that she pretended to be pregnant, but this was easily disproved. She was taken to Tyburn in a mourning coach rather than a wagon, with soldiers along the route – perhaps as a mark of respect, but more likely to ensure that members of her former gang did not attempt a rescue.

Chapter Six

The Rebel Collection – Pirates, Witches, Megalomaniacs, Exhibitionists

BINZ, Dorothea 1920–47

Aged just nineteen at the outbreak of the Second World War, German-born Dorothea chose the SS as a way of escaping her dull farming family and her dull life as a maidservant. Her new job, as a guard in the nearby concentration camp at Ravensbruck, seems to have filled her with pride rather than horror. Ravensbruck was the only German camp exclusively for women, with some 50,000 killed and closer to 100,000 tortured. Dorothea was one of well over 3,000 women guards.

A blue-eyed blonde, who became known as the beautiful bitch, Dorothea Binz had chosen the perfect role for her sadistic nature. This had not really surfaced before she took on this – to many – deeply unpleasant role, although she had been a young member of the female branch of Hitler Youth (the League of German Girls). She was remembered and reviled by survivors as having had no qualms about handing out beatings, or throwing icy water over skeletal, scantily clad women already suffering from overwork, the cold weather and malnutrition.

One of her pleasures in life, it seems, was watching prisoners being hanged, when the opportunity arose. It seems she also liked using her heavy boots to stomp on women who had fallen to the ground and was known to use a whip and even a pickaxe to inflict fatal wounds. If questioned about her behaviour, her reaction was simply that the prisoners were a 'burden on the Fatherland' and needed brutal treatment to 'keep them in check' especially if they were 'Russian swine' from the Red Army. Such an attitude actually led to her being promoted – first of all as the overseer of the brutal punishments being dished out in what was called the Bunker, and then through the ranks to Chief Wardress, responsible for training other female guards, many of whom were sent to Auschwitz.

Dorothea's 'boyfriend' was a married SS officer, Edmund Brauning, with whom she had a lot in common. They enjoyed watching women being flogged and apparently kissed and canoodled in full view of them, a habit often mentioned by the prosecution when she finally came to trial in May 1945. She had fled Ravensbruck on her bicycle after Russian troops arrived and was captured by the British and imprisoned before being tried with other SS personnel in Hamburg at one of the seven war crime trials in the town. It was the famous British executioner, Albert Pierrepoint, who ended her life in Hamelin prison, aged just twenty-seven, the youngest by far of the three Nazi women hanged there on 2 May 1947.

BONNY, Anne c.1700–c.1782 (?) and READ, Mary c.1695–1721

Two of the few women who took to piracy, their story would make a great film. Anne was born, illegitimately, to a successful lawyer in Ireland who took her to the American colonies when the parochial locals were scandalised by

Copper engraving c. 1724 from *The Life of Mary Read in A General History of the Pyrates: From Their First Rise and Settlement in the Island of Providence, to the Present Time. With the Remarkable Actions and Adventures of the Two Female Pyrates Mary Read and Anne Bonny. To Which is Added. A Short Abstract of the Statute and Civil Law, in Relation to Pyracy* by Daniel Defoe and Charles Johnson (2nd ed.), published by T. Warner, London (pp. plate facing p. 157, engraved by Benjamin Cole (1695–1766). Public domain per commons.wikimedia.org her dressing up as a boy to pose as his assistant, rather than his daughter. You would think they would be more upset at an earlier scandal when she was said to have stabbed (and possibly killed) a servant girl!

Having made a success in America as a merchant, her father then disowned her when she married a penniless sailor in 1718. The marriage did not last because Anne became enamoured with the already notorious John Rackham (aka Calico Jack). It seems she was sentenced to a flogging for her adultery, but Jack managed to free her. She left her husband and went to sea with Jack, becoming pregnant with their child before joining his crew – dressed in far more practical male clothing.

She met English-born Mary Read on board, who had been dressed as a boy by her mother so that she could earn more money. Mary had been a cadet in Belgium, still disguised as a boy, until she revealed herself to a Flemish soldier and ended up marrying him. In her case, her husband died and she set off for a new life in the West Indies but it appears that her ship – along with Mary – was captured by pirates. It seems Mary was more than happy to join them rather than put up any resistance – and the story goes that even Mary did not realise Anne was also a woman until she tried to seduce her.

Anne and Mary were part of a violent, foul-mouthed crew who did not just pillage and loot other vessels, but tortured or murdered anyone in the way, indulging in drunken orgies before and after. John Rackham's sloop was finally captured off Jamaica in 1720 and the men – who it seemed were too drunk to resist arrest, leaving the strongest resistance to the two women! – were all hanged. Calico Jack's body was suspended from a gibbet at the entrance to Kingston Harbour, bound in chains. The two women were tried separately, and it is from the records of the trial that most of the details about their astonishing adventures came to light. They escaped the noose because both were examined and found to be pregnant.

The records of Mary's death, from a fever while in prison, give a date of April 1721. But as for Anne … some historians are convinced she escaped, others that she was 'rescued' by her rich father who found her a respectable husband, but the general consensus was that she lived to a ripe old age, the mother of as many as ten children.

BOUDICCA (or BOADICEA), Queen of the Iceni c.25–c.61

If anyone had cause to be 'bad', surely it was Boudicca. With an aristocratic background, she was married to Prasutagus, ruler of the Iceni people of East Anglia, at the time of the Roman invasion in 43 AD. Her husband was allowed to continue to 'rule' until his death in about 60 perhaps because he made Nero co-heir to his kingdom. But then, rather than showing any gratitude, his lands and household were plundered by the Romans. Boudicca lost her land, her property, and was subjected to a public flogging as well as the trauma of both her daughters being raped.

The red hair should have warned the Romans that they were not going to walk away from this defilement. The Roman historian Dio Cassius wrote of her as tall and fierce with 'the tawniest hair' – her long red hair representing

Boudicca.

high status at the time, later representing witchcraft. The Iceni, now led by Boudicca, rebelled, and were joined by other local tribes.

Boudicca's warriors first captured the Roman capital of Camulodunum (Colchester), and then stormed the twenty-year-old Londinium (London) and Verulamium (St Albans), leaving the towns pillaged and in flames, with desecrated Roman cemeteries. The Roman governor, Suetonius, who had been on a campaign in Wales, was provoked into assembling an army of 10,000 to take on the avenging Britons, the battle taking place in the Midlands, probably in the vicinity of Nuneaton.

Before the battle, Boudicca drove her chariot around her tribes, accompanied by her daughters, pointing out what they were fighting for and taunting them with the shame of slavery if they were not victorious. Tennyson may have described her in his eponymous poem as a 'mad and maddening' avenger but he also refers to her 'evil tyrannies and 'pitiless avarice'. There is no doubt that Boudicca was a savage warrior, with her army committing bestial atrocities such as cutting off the breasts of noble women and sewing them to their mouths (allowing for Roman exaggeration).

In spite of the Britons' brave fight, they suffered massive casualties early on in the confrontation – their long swords were of no real use except in close combat and they were out-manoeuvred by the Romans and their javelins. Records show that only 400 Romans were lost, but 80,000 Britons died, although the accuracy of these figures has often been the subject of scholarly debate.

Although not killed in battle, Boudicca took poison before she could be captured and she may have even poisoned her daughters to save them suffering. The location of her burial site remains a mystery, with a variety of locations possible. Was she buried with the Iceni treasures? If she was, she has kept their location a secret not just from her enemies but from generations of historians and archaeologists.

CAMPBELL, Fanny Eighteenth Century

While Fanny Campbell has been fictionalised in stories about the American Revolution, there seems to be no doubt that there was indeed such an individual even though no birth or death records have yet come to light. Stories of her childhood tell of her being well educated but able to row a boat and shoot a panther.

She is recorded as being among the first captains to take private craft into service against the British at the time. Her reasons were not political or patriotic, however, they were the actions of a lovesick woman whose childhood sweetheart, William Lovell, had been jailed after escaping from capture by a pirate ship, ending with him also being charged with piracy.

From Massachusetts, she had dressed as a man to secure a position as a deckhand on the *Constance*, where she led a mutiny against the

FANNY CAMPBELL,
THE FEMALE PIRATE CAPTAIN.

Portrait of the Female Pirate.

BY LIEUTENANT MURRAY.

BOSTON:
PUBLISHED BY F. GLEASON, 1 1-2 TREMONT ROW.
1845.

Scanned from 1844 novel *Fanny Campbell, The Female Pirate* by M.M.Balou, published by F. Gleason, Boston, U.S.A.

existing captain, who the crew suspected was on his way to press them into the British Navy. As Captain Channing, she kept her gender secret, succeeding in her rebellion and she was confirmed as the commander, which meant that she – and the crew – were all now wanted as pirates. The *Constance* managed to overpower another ship en route to the Cuban jail where William was being kept, adding to the notoriety of the ship and its occupants.

The *Constance*, with help from the ship she had captured (the *George*), managed to rescue not just William but ten other Americans, and took to sea as war broke out between England and America. This meant that Fanny was able to escape the stigma of piracy because she (or, as she was then regarded, 'he') could legally command a private warship as a legitimate privateer in the American cause – an opportunity she willingly took on, capturing at least one British man-of-war in the ensuing naval battles. But although William continued as a privateer once he and Fanny were married, she was soon relegated to the traditional role of mother and home-maker.

The American writer, Kathy Warnes, tells of some of the children ignoring the 'cutlass in their mother's closet' while others 'pointed it out with pride'. Their confusion is understandable. There is no doubt that piracy was – and still is come to that – against the law, regardless of its motivation, but this particular female is unlikely to be regarded as wicked … however, if it had not been for the start of the American War of Independence (from the British and especially the British taxes), things might have been very different.

CANARY, Martha Jane (aka Calamity Jane) 1852–1903

Martha Jane was orphaned – along with around five younger siblings – by the age of thirteen, her parents having been involved in petty crime and often destitute. The family had moved from Princeton, Missouri to Salt Lake City by that time and the illiterate Martha was obliged to take any paid work she could find to survive. This often meant pretending to be a young man, which she could get away with because of her height and build and taking on men's work. It helped that she was already a good markswoman and a fearless horsewoman who quickly acquired a taste for poker, whisky and tobacco.

She was only sixteen when she got her first job as a bullwhacker (driver)

Martha Jane Canary.

for a wagon train and she quickly gained a reputation as a tough cookie who was probably the first woman to get away with being served in an American saloon. There are various versions of how she got her nickname, Calamity, perhaps the most authentic being her habit of stirring up an argument wherever she went.

The bravado stories she told of her skirmishes with the American Indians, rescuing a runaway stage coach and of scouting for General Custer, are no doubt exaggerated. Her ability as a raconteur was just another skill that impressed the men she met, including Wild Bill Hickok, who admired her nearly as much as she admired him.

The two characters, who had met in 1872, had equal reputations for their foul mouths and gambling skills and they shared the same taste in clothes; heavily fringed buckskins and Stetson hats. Their exuberant arrival with their wagon train in Deadwood Gulch in 1876 at the time of the Gold Rush was headlined by the local paper, the *Black Hills Daily Times*, which described Martha as a 'yelling and whooping Amazonian'.

There does not seem to have been a romantic relationship between the two, perhaps partly because Martha was often described as having ruddy skin and stringy, unwashed hair, in keeping with her shabby clothes. One of the few times she wore a dress was when she went to the undertakers following Bill Hickok's death in 1876 , after he was shot during a poker game.

The years following Bill's death have been described variously by different biographers. She seems to have stayed on in Deadwood for a while, as there are accounts of her nursing patients there during an outbreak of smallpox. It is said she then moved away, married and had a daughter, running a hotel for a while. Certainly, she turns up as her old self in 1895 when she joined Buffalo Bill's Wild West Show, using her skills with a gun and a horse on tour with the show. However, she so often became drunk and disorderly that this was not her finest hour and when the tours finally came to an end she declined further into alcoholism.

Not too surprisingly, Martha died not long after, in August 1903. She had become so notorious in her own lifetime that her hair had to be protected by a wire cage to stop souvenir hunters cutting off pieces as she lay in the coffin at the undertaker's. Her funeral in Deadwood, where she was buried next to Wild Bill Hickok, as per her wishes, was the largest held there for a woman.

CIXI, Empress Dowager (also known as Tsu-Hzi) 1835–1908

Few women in history have inspired such a diverse range of views as China's Cixi. Her family were involved in government in some way, but little is known of her until the age of sixteen when she features as one of many concubines of Emperor Hsien-Feng. As concubine, she would be taken, naked, to his bed by court eunuchs as and when needed.

Already an expensively garbed, though diminutive, member of the court, her status improved vastly, however, when she bore his only son in 1856. Now she began offering possibly unwanted advice to the emperor, because on his deathbed he set up an

Empress Dowager CIXI.

eight-man regency to run the country, diminishing her influence. However, when her son was crowned emperor in 1861, Cixi launched a palace coup. She accused the regents of forging the emperor's will and falsely seizing control and had Minister Su Shun beheaded; two regents committed suicide, starting the route to her reputation for being ruthless. Although theoretically sharing power with the Emperor's No. 1 concubine, and acting as joint Empress Dowagers, only Cixi had any interest in politics.

Cixi's popularity declined even further when she increased taxes to sustain the grandeur of the royal palace and her own lifestyle. She also succeeded in undermining the influence of the dead Emperor's brother. There are further stories of her 'selling' court positions in return for 'donations.'

Her son, Tongzhi, died as a teenager from smallpox, already having succumbed to venereal disease thanks to the debauched life he led at court. His wife committed suicide by overdosing on opium – possibly with Cixi's help. With Cixi's influence, and against tradition, he was succeeded by her three-year-old nephew, Guangxu, who she promptly adopted. This seems to have provoked more rivalry from Niuhuru, the other regent or

Empress Dowager, perhaps because Guangxu preferred Niuhuru, but she conveniently died after eating some rice cakes sent to her by Cixi.

This meant Cixi effectively ruled alone as regent, apparently feared by the young emperor, Guangxu, until he reached his majority when Cixi was fifty-five and ready to retire. However, she did not disappear off the scene as she was concerned about his Westernised views and the two crossed swords politically. She actually managed to manoeuvre the situation so that he was deposed and imprisoned in 1898, with all his attendants banished, or, worse, killed. Cixi was back in control.

Her biggest mistake was supporting the anti-foreign, anti-Christian Boxer rebellion that rocked China in 1899. When foreign troops arrived on her doorstep, she was forced to flee, disguised as a peasant. She took the emperor with her, even though he was distressed by her ordering the death of his favourite concubine.

They returned when peace was declared in 1901, but not to the same power and glamour they had previously enjoyed. They both died in 1908, the emperor in agony, showing symptoms beyond those of the liver complaint he had and cursing his aunt on his deathbed. Was it arsenic that in fact ended his life? Was Cixi responsible for his death, too, to ensure he did not make a comeback without her? She died the next day, weak and prepared for the end, returning China to its male-dominated autocracy and its last emperor.

Although buried with ceremony, twenty years later any remaining respect was undermined by whoever dynamited her tomb, stole her teeth and jewellery and threw her body aside.

DE MEDICI, Catherine 1519–89

Italian born, Catherine's aristocratic parents died when she was a baby. It was her uncle who arranged her marriage to the King of France's second son when they were fourteen, although there was no child of the marriage until ten years later. Her husband, the Duke of Orleans, was crowned Henry II of France in 1547 but died in a jousting accident in 1559, their eldest son, Francis, taking on the reins, in spite of the efforts of a military uprising. This was prevented by the royal army, with fifty-seven leaders hanged or beheaded in front of Catherine and her family. When Francis died a year later, her second son, Charles, took over, aged just ten, leaving control effectively in Catherine's hands.

The French Wars of Religion meant that the Catholic Catherine was at loggerheads with the Protestant Huguenots. Although she arranged the marriage of her daughter to Henry, the Huguenot King of Navarre in 1572, Henry's mother died suddenly during negotiations and Catherine was suspected of poisoning her. At the wedding, the Huguenot leader, Coligny, who had been suspected of plotting to overthrow Charles, was shot and the plan to have him assassinated was thought to have been devised by Catherine.

Catherine de Medici.

As panic and fighting broke out, Catholic troops moved in, with Charles apparently persuaded of Coligny's treachery. Extended looting and fighting flared up throughout Paris, with Catherine again blamed for ordering the troops to attack. Two thousand people died, most of them Protestants, including women and children, many of whom were gathered to celebrate the royal wedding. The injured Coligny was one of the early victims, as were other Huguenot leaders. The date was 24 August, St Bartholomew's Day, hence the event being recorded in history as the Bartholomew's Day Massacre. With civil war continuing, further massacres followed in the provinces.

Catherine continued to play a central role behind the throne when Charles, too, died, succeeded by her favourite son, Henry III, in 1574. She witnessed the execution of the leaders of yet another Huguenot uprising when Henry briefly took over the Polish throne, but some say that what she really wanted was an end to civil war. It was the way she worked to achieve this, if this indeed was her aim, that has left her with a reputation for Machiavellian revenge and ruthlessness.

Her husband had had a mistress for the whole of their marriage, Diane de Poitiers, twenty years his senior. Some historians have considered whether this led to Catherine's intolerance and bitterness, but mistresses were much more accepted then than now in royal circles. She survived her husband by thirty years, dying after dancing at the marriage of one of her grand-daughters, but with conflict between Huguenots and Catholics still raging.

DESHAYES, Catherine (La Voisin) c.1640–80

Although nothing is known of Catherine's childhood in France, it seems that as a child she was taught fortune telling, one of many barefoot beggars earning pennies from this 'skill', which she developed to a superior standard. She called it into play when her jeweller husband, Monvoisin, faced financial difficulties, practising palm-reading and face-reading for a fee.

La Voisin took a magician as one of her lovers, and, between them, they acquired a host of superstitious, gullible and above all else, wealthy, Parisian clients. She began to practice witchcraft (with the help of a renegade priest who would arrange black masses) with one spell involving the need for the blood of a child. Midwifery, including abortion, was added to her skill set, along with providing rejuvenating creams and skin tonics based on herbal preparations. This progressed to love potions whose ingredients included moles' teeth, toads' bones, human blood, iron filings and dead beetles!

There is a theory that she also established a home for unwed mothers, providing her with a stockpile of sacrificial infants!

As La Voisin's profitable business empire grew, clients became interested in her aptitude for providing poisons so they could remove rivals in love or in politics. The death of the duchess of Orleans was attributed to poison and a commission appointed in 1679 to investigate similar deaths, when it was revealed that Louis XIV's mistress, Madame de Montespan, had been planning his demise.

The police interviewed La Voisin's daughter when they heard that Montespan had visited La Voisin first to buy spells to undermine – or even kill – any potential rival by, for example, impregnating her clothing with arsenic and sulphur. Then, when that failed, she was in the market for aphrodisiacs.

Anyone found plotting against the King was liable to be imprisoned or flogged at best, or sent to the scaffold at worst , but those of the status of Madame de Montespan avoided disgrace so that the King himself was not involved in proceedings. Investigations found a network of Parisians who distributed poisons, including La Voisin, and the King ordered that the whole network be exterminated. This scandal became known as the Poison Affair, an almost hysterical pursuit of murder suspects as the result of witchcraft and poisoning. Those with private influence were lucky, while other innocents were apparently imprisoned for life.

La Voisin's was one of the early prosecutions. She was arrested on her way home from church and at her trial apparently stated that she had sacrificed more than 2,500 children who had their throats slit at Black Sabbaths. After spending a year in prison, she confessed to further crimes such as abortions after being tortured – her legs systematically crushed. This treatment also resulted in her implicating a list of clients which reads like a French Who's Who; the Duc de Luxembourg, the Comtesse de Soissons and many more.

Unsurprisingly, she was convicted of witchcraft and poisoning and burned in public in Paris. Legend has it that she went to her death singing offensive songs. But a sad ending for a woman looking to earn a crust.

FLOWER, Joan c.1565–1619 (and her daughters)

Joan and her daughters, Margaret and Philippa, were servants of the Earl of Rutland at Belvoir Castle near Grantham in Lincolnshire. When they were dismissed for stealing, the Earl's whole family became ill, suffering convulsions, the eldest son, Henry, dying as a result. The Earl and his wife blamed Joan Flower (an atheist who had boasted of her affinity with familiars, including her cat, Rutterkin) and her daughters, known to have threatened revenge on the family.

All three were arrested at Christmastime, 1618. This was of course at the time when witchcraft came to prominence thanks to James I's fondness for the subject. The three were taken to Lincoln jail, where they were questioned. It seems that the unkempt and foul-mouthed Joan decided she would prove her innocence by eating bread not blessed by the Eucharist – if it choked her, the theory was that it proved she was guilty of casting a spell over the family. But choke her – to death – it did!

Her daughters were subjected to five weeks of deprivation and torture until they confessed. They passed the blame onto their mother, who was said to have cast her spell by dipping Henry's glove in boiling water, rubbing it along Rutterkin's back before pricking and burying it, accompanied by incantations to ensure that Henry and the glove disintegrated simultaneously.

There was, predictably, little 'evidence' to support accusations of witchcraft against the sisters, but they were generally regarded locally as obnoxious and of low morals, which seems to have been enough. Uneducated and unable to defend themselves, they were tried, found guilty, and hanged at Lincoln the following March, along with three other local women they had incriminated along the way.

The Earl and Countess of Rutland had their sons' tomb inscribed 'Two sonnes – both who dyed in their infancy by wicked practice and sorcerye' even though their younger son had died long after Henry. The tomb is in Bottesford Church in Leicestershire, just over the border with Lincolnshire. As for Joan, she is buried on the crossroads in the village of Ancaster, a common practice with witches, so they would not know which way to go if they returned. Joan and her daughters were just three of the 100,000 or so people sentenced to death for witchcraft in Britain between the fifteenth and eighteenth centuries, many of them victims of little more than a local vendetta.

GRESE, Irma 1923–45

The women who adopted the Nazi creed were often more sadistic than the men. Irma Grese was a prime example: from joining the League of German Girls (the female version of Hitler Youth) to working in the concentration camps, she revelled in her role as, eventually, the 'beautiful beast of Belsen'.

From an unremarkable agricultural family in the village of Wrechen (north of Berlin), the attractive blonde Irma was actually sent to work at Ravensbruck camp at the age of fifteen by her local

Irma Grese.

Labour Exchange! Perhaps they had an insight into her personality, because she had found her calling. By nineteen, she was a Senior SS Supervisor there, and also worked at Auschwitz before ending up at Belsen.

In 1945, when Belsen was liberated by the British, she was one of the guards arrested. She tried pleading not guilty to the charges of murder and ill treatment of prisoners, but there was too much evidence and too many witnesses for this plea to be taken seriously. Witnesses spoke of Irma patrolling the camp with her German shepherds. The skeletal prisoners were set upon by the dogs for any excuse and then they were kicked with her heavy boots until they were dead or dying. It seems she took a particular delight in whipping and slashing the breasts of women who were well-endowed or whipping their faces if some beauty remained. Another of her pleasures was to send women on errands outside the barbed wire enclosure which meant they were shot down by guards. She claimed that the pistol she carried – in addition to the whip – was only for show, but she had been seen using it to shoot anyone who tried to escape the gas chamber lines.

Some of the witnesses at her trial seemed to feel that she derived sexual pleasure at her acts of cruelty, although she was also said to have had SS lovers including Josef Mengele and an abortion. Additionally, Irma was not averse to emotional cruelty, taunting the prisoners about whether it was their turn for the gas chamber or not and then apparently changing her mind. At some stage, she had admitted to regarding the prisoners not just as enemies of the state but as sub-human rubbish and saw nothing wrong in what she was doing. There again, she was a very young woman given a free hand to kill and torture thousands of innocent people, even though there were 'rules' against their mistreatment, woefully disregarded.

Her notoriety is partly as a result of the three lampshades found in her room, made of human skin. But this may well be one of those added-on stories after the event. The story that she planned a career in the movies post-war is more likely.

Albert Pierrepoint was flown over to Hamelin prison specially to execute Irma and thirteen others on, rather appropriately, Friday 13 December. She and the other two women similarly sentenced spent the night before their execution singing Nazi and German patriotic songs. She was the youngest to die, her last word, once the white cap was on her head, being '*Schnell*' (Quickly).

HARI, Mata 1876–1917

Dutch born Margaretha Zelle (her real name) had a comfortable life thanks to her hat-maker father, until he went bankrupt – and walked out – when she was thirteen. She started training as a teacher but got involved with the college proprietor and was promptly dismissed, reconciled to marriage as her only future.

With a view to that end, she replied to a personal ad from a 'Dutch army captain' seeking a wife. He was twenty-two years her senior but she accepted his proposal, not realising he was an alcoholic and a wife-beater. Things looked a bit more promising

Mata Hari.

when he was transferred to Java as a garrison commander, after their son was born, a place Margaretha embraced and where their daughter was born in 1898.

However, both children were poisoned by someone with a grudge against her husband and her son died as a result. The couple divorced (a rare event at the time) and her husband took their daughter, known as Non, but Margaretha promised her that she would come back for her when she was rich.

Arriving in Paris in 1905, penniless, her striking looks meant she secured work quickly as an artists' model, but it didn't pay the sort of money she needed to get her daughter back. So, because she had enjoyed joining in the dancing with the natives of Java and because anything 'oriental' was in fashion in France, the idea of exotic dancing was born – and she became an overnight sensation. Her costumes became more and more daring, the most famous being the 'seven veils' which were removed in a slow striptease down to a body-stocking. She worked in Paris venues for nearly ten years and then branched out to the other European capitals.

Although she now could fetch Non, she knew that the lifestyle was unsuitable for her daughter, but this was not her only problem. War had broken out, decadence was less desirable, she was approaching forty … One offer she did accept was a six-month season performing at the Metropole in Berlin in 1916 – entertaining German officers in between dances. Amongst these was the Berlin Police Chief, Traugott von Jagow.

When she decided to return home, she was interviewed by the French Secret Service who regarded her lifestyle – and companions – as 'suspicious' but this just prompted her to return to Paris, where she was followed by two detectives. Meanwhile, Mata (as she called herself, *Mata Hari* being Indonesian for eye of the day) had taken a young Russian lover, a pilot flying for the French. Her request to access the military zone where he was stationed was intercepted by French police who interviewed her, still suspecting that she was a spy. Mata convinced them otherwise, and they made her quite an offer – one million francs if she spied for France! She may not have been a spy before that meeting, but she could not refuse such riches.

Even when travelling through Britain, MI5 mistook her for a German spy (!) but it was in Madrid that she seduced the German military attaché, who, although he appeared very indiscreet with his pillow talk, actually fed her false information. As a result, she was not paid the sum promised and was arrested by the French. After numerous interviews, she admitted – fatally – to taking money from one of the Germans to spy on France, but had not carried out the mission; she had just kept the money.

She was tried by a military tribunal in Paris in 1917, her morals on trial as much as her possible spying activities, and convicted on very shaky evidence of causing the deaths of many thousands of French soldiers. Facing the firing squad, she refused to wear a blindfold and blew a last, theatrical kiss before the shots rang out. A performer to the end.

ISABELLA OF FRANCE c.1295–1358

Isabella was born in Paris, the youngest child of Philip IV of France and Joan I of Navarre, and married Edward II of England in 1308, a political alliance attempting to resolve the French/English conflicts. Unhappily for this beautiful and very young bride, Edward favoured male members of his court, and was almost certainly bi-sexual. In fact, upon their arrival in Dover from France, after their marriage, Edward was more interested in bestowing affection on his then lover, Piers Gaveston, apparently giving him the couple's wedding presents! It was Gaveston who drew more attention at their coronation than Isabella, dressing and behaving as if *he* was the guest of honour and turning the occasion into a fiasco.

Isabella of France, portrayed here in a sculpture by Cedric Amey in the St Louis de Poissy Priory.

The barons, and Isabella of course, were disgusted not just with Edward's behaviour but with his neglect of duty and saw to it that his biggest favourites were exiled, or worse; Gaveston was executed in 1312. Baronial revolts continued, however, some of which Edward gained enough support to crush, with leaders being executed.

When Edward managed to recall several of his exiled favourites who, together, seized property and disregarded the law, Isabella finally returned to France in 1325, her brother seizing Edward's French possessions. This visit may also have had something to do with what became an affair with Roger Mortimer, who had escaped to France from the Tower of London after being imprisoned during one of the many revolts against Edward. Whether they knew each other before her return is not proven (but is likely) and nor is whether she actually helped him to escape.

The couple plotted to depose Edward, gathering an army which invaded England in 1326. With the help of family in Holland, who provided a number of war ships, this small army (mostly mercenaries) landed in England to find that Edward was offering a reward for their deaths. Isabella offered twice the amount for the capture of Hugh le Despenser the younger, another of her husband's favourites that he had restored to the court, and Despenser was indeed captured, hanged, drawn and quartered.

The invasion was a success and Edward was deposed by parliament. Isabella and Roger ruled as co-regents after Edward was unpleasantly tortured and murdered in Berkeley Castle in 1327 with a hot poker in his rectum. The fourteen-year-old Prince of Wales took the throne as Edward III, with Isabella predictably suspected (again unproven) of issuing the order for Edward II's death, if not the manner of it. Wealth and honours were subsequently heaped on Roger Mortimer but he began to enjoy his new power and exert force to increase it.

Isabella's son, Edward, was not happy with her regency and headed up a coup in 1330, with both Isabella and her lover imprisoned. This seems to have been provoked by the murder of his uncle, the Earl of Kent, allegedly orchestrated – again – by Isabella and Roger. Mortimer was executed for treason a month later, but Isabella's life was spared by her son, and she retired to Castle Rising in Norfolk, later taking holy orders. She died in 1358 and was buried in her wedding dress with Edward's heart in a casket, but in the church where Roger Mortimer was buried.

Was Isabella indeed the instigator of a number of executions, including that of her husband? Or a convenient scapegoat? She led one of the most successful invasions of England in history, and has inherited the title She-Wolf of France, not a title that could be attributed to someone squeaky clean, that's for certain. At best, however badly treated, she turned a blind eye to regicide, earning her inheritance as an unloved and unmourned royal.

JEZEBEL c.900–c.843 BC

Born to the Phoenician King Ethbaal, Jezebel was brought up in the luxurious palaces of Sidon. Her father and his people were superstitious and pagan, following some cruel and licentious rites and Jezebel was not only an idol worshipper, but may have been trained as a priestess, following in her father's footsteps.

When she was nineteen(ish) she was married, in a political alliance, to the much older King Ahab of Israel. This meant that she could continue her lavish lifestyle though in a more conservative fashion, and she installed 450 priests to serve the god Baal and 400 to serve the goddess Astarte (both

"Jezebel and Ahab meeting Elijah in Naboth's Vineyard" – a Giclee print by Sir Frank Bernard Dicksee (1853–1928).

figures linked to fertility). The Israeli people thought her Phoenician ways were not just shocking, but verging on insulting.

An influential enemy was the prophet Elijah, who organised the slaughter of her priests, and Jezebel vowed to crush him, in part by slaughtering his priests in turn. He escaped to Mount Sinai, while, in the meantime, Jezebel ordered the death of her neighbour Naboth (by stoning) because Jewish law forbade him from handing over his family vineyard to her husband – and she convinced the townspeople that she was in the right. Elijah, with obvious concerns about Jezebel's power over the people, returned to confront the King, predicting famine, drought and the death of Ahab and his family because they were openly opposing the Jewish religion. While this seems to have frightened Ahab, it had no effect on Jezebel in spite of Elijah telling her that she would end her life trampled by horses and eaten by dogs.

She had given birth to two sons and a daughter by Ahab, but when Ahab died in around 853 BC, Elijah's successor, Elisha, proclaimed Jehu, a military commander, as the new King of Israel and ordered him to eradicate the House of Ahab. Jehu first murdered Jezebel's son, Jehoram, who had taken over as King, and then made his way to Jezebel's palace. She did not try to escape but used kohl on her eyes (connected with harlotry at the time), dressed herself in her finest and most alluring gown and styled her hair in preparation, then waited at an upper window. Whether this was a ritual preparation for death or whether she had prepared to seduce Jehu is where the fact and fiction become impossible to unpick.

It seems that Jehu and his men wasted no time in arranging for Jezebel's eunuchs to throw her out of the window. Elijah's prophecy apparently came true in that she was trampled to death by horses. When the new Israeli King Jehu latterly sent troops to fetch the body of Jezebel for burial, all that had been uneaten by the dogs – again, as per Elijah – were the skull and the feet and the palms of her hands (Kings 9:35).

MARY I (Bloody Mary) 1516–58

At marriageable age, Mary was rather tiny and thin and, although she was musical and intelligent, visits from prospective European husbands did not have a favourable outcome. She was forced to separate from her mother, Catherine of Aragon, in 1532 when the marriage between her and Henry VIII was declared illegal and Mary's household was reduced substantially to a size appropriate for a 'royal bastard'.

It wasn't until 1544 that King Henry re-established her as heir apparent to Edward, but her adherence to Catholicism was a problem once he came to the throne in 1547 and she was

Mary I.

kept virtually under house arrest. The King showed his displeasure at her behaviour – for example, celebrating Mass – by sending a series of influential messengers, but these she dismissed with scorn. She told them she would readily die for her faith and would fend for herself if necessary. When the royal chamberlain visited her to inform her that she was to be stripped of her title of princess, her response was rebellious. She declared that she had no doubt that she was 'the King's true daughter, born in good and lawful matrimony'.

Feeling her life was in danger, she made plans in 1550 to escape to Holland – a Catholic country – in a ship sent by her uncle, Emperor Charles V, to the Essex coast. However, a peasant uprising had meant an increase in the watch and such a departure would be challenged. The next plan was that the Emperor's warships would ride at anchor in the Blackwater Estuary, ostensibly to attack pirates; from there an innocent-looking corn boat would make contact with her via the port at Maldon but suspicions were somehow aroused resulting in the arrest of the corn boat.

Hostility to Protestantism and to the new Prayer book was not a good idea, following on the heels of insurgency in Norfolk and Cornwall and pressure was put on Mary to return to court, far from the sea. She pleaded ill-health and did not budge until March 1551 when she was ordered to King Edward's presence, where he berated her for hearing Mass, though this seemed to make little difference. But he died of consumption in 1553 and Mary proclaimed herself Queen, rejecting the claim of Lady Jane Grey. A delicate, domestic, rather unhappy individual, dedicated to her faith, she became the first English woman to be crowned without a civil war breaking out.

Following Edward's short reign – and Lady Jane Grey's even briefer attempt to take her place – Mary's reign (from 1553) saw the return of the country to Catholicism. Part of her grand plan – after Jane's execution – was to put down those who revolted against her and persecute Protestants. It is this latter trait that earned her the name of Bloody Mary.

It was only after her marriage to Philip II of Spain in 1554 that her religious fanaticism and murderous nature surfaced. The marriage was arguably the most unpopular royal marriage in English history, Spain being no friend to England. But she ignored her father-in-law's advice to tread gently in her religious reform and her religious zeal created 273 Protestant Marian martyrs. With the help of the equally fanatical Bishop of London, Edward

Bonner, many Protestant bishops were deposed. Cranmer and Latimer were burned at the stake. Protestants faced fire or exile as the Mass returned to the churches. She also damaged her reputation with non-religious members of the public by excluding Princess Elizabeth from the succession and forcing her into near-solitary confinement.

Thankfully, Mary's reign was limited to five years. She produced no children although some sources reveal that she thought she was pregnant shortly before her death, while others attribute the 'symptoms' to stomach cancer. There was dancing in the street at the news of her death in 1558.

MASCHIN, Draga 1864–1903

One of the few queens in a book such as this and probably the least well-known, is Draga, Queen of Serbia from 1900–1903. Before 1900, as a young widow, she had been lady-in-waiting to Queen Natalie, but was known to be a courtesan (probably the mistress of Natalie's husband, King Milan, amongst others) who frequented disreputable areas. This lifestyle may not have been that surprising, given that her mother was a low-life drunk and her father had mental health issues.

While some sources describe her as unattractive, she obviously had qualities because she was able to attract Prince Alexander, twelve years her junior and a frequenter of local brothels. One story indicates that Draga had saved Alexander from drowning as a young teenager, which, if true, may have some bearing on her attraction. When his tyrannical father, under pressure from influential Serbians, abdicated in 1889, Alexander was thirteen but became more and more interested in the salacious side of life. His first act as King, aged seventeen, was to exile his disapproving mother and recall his father to office in the Army.

After a few years of hedonism and in spite of his having a sexually transmitted disease, Alexander announced – on New Year's Day 1900 – that he would marry, to keep the government officials happy. His choice of bride stunned his family, the officials and the public. An older, penniless widow regarded as the Queen of Whores – Draga Maschin. This was the last straw for the largely anti-royal populace and for the Government who resigned *en masse* when Alexander refused to change his mind. The marriage took place with little ceremony and a complete absence of celebration other than between Alexander and Draga. By now, Milan was accusing Draga of being a Russian spy and blackmailing letters were pouring in from her clients, threatening to take their experiences to the press.

Draga, foolishly, thought that announcing her pregnancy would 'help' matters but as she was generally known to be infertile, this announcement carried no weight and just exacerbated the anti-Draga faction. There were stories that she had planned to secretly introduce a changeling, thus securing her power. This idea failing, she then came up with an Heir Apparent of her own choice; her brother. Her control over Alexander was such that he agreed to issue a royal decree in his favour. The Serbians became apoplectic.

Draga ignored them, going on a spending spree using money allocated for a drainage system to buy a yacht and Parisian outfits ... not surprisingly, opponents of the marriage, and of Draga in particular, began to plot their undoing. Plans were made to depose Alexander and expel Draga from Serbia, but some conspirators wanted something more final. Following an extravagant royal gala in the Belgrade palace, the fury of these conspirators became extreme, resulting in the royal couple being sought out and shot in their rooms. The plotters emptied their revolvers into the bodies and trampled them underfoot, so hated were they.

Draga had attained the power she apparently sought, but not for long. Her short but sensational reign made the king and his consort the laughing stock of Europe.

MITFORD, Unity 1914–48

Unity and her sisters were born into luxury; their father, the bigoted Lord Redesdale, owned a Canadian goldmine – the Swastika goldmine. The swastika was to play a part in Unity's life, and note her middle name 'Valkyrie' as a nod to the German composer, Wagner. There was a large house in Rutland Gate, London and a family estate in the Cotswolds.

Unity did not appreciate such assets. Mainly home educated, she was expelled from at least one school for flouting the rules and was easily bored. At eighteen, at the end of her debutante season, she was introduced to Oswald Mosley by her married sister, Diana, who was having an affair with the married fascist leader. She, too, succumbed to his 'charms' and is said to have lost her virginity to him on a billiard table during one of the season's balls, the occasion said to have been encouraged by Diana.

Having joined the British Union of Fascists, she could be seen in the local villages wearing the swastika and greeting people with the Nazi salute. Thanks to her interest in the explicitly sexual works of the German Hieronymus Bosch, an artist she emulated, she enrolled at the London County Council School of Art in 1933. This was the same year that she travelled to the Nuremberg party rally. She was the only woman in the British delegation and featured on the official Nazi brochure in tweed suit and black shirt, with her black gloved hand held up in the famous salute.

A year later, she managed to persuade her parents to send her to a finishing school in Munich, perhaps not too surprising given her father's approval of Aryan ascendancy. She wanted to learn the German language to prepare her for the meeting she had planned with Hitler. This didn't happen in reality until February 1935, when he finally called her over to his restaurant table, aware of her constant presence and possibly intrigued that she did not fall at his feet like so many others.

In the meantime, some of her biographers, including those with credible Mitford family sources, have written of her enjoying protracted orgies with as many as six SS officers at one time. These orgies involved Unity being tied to a bed and being blindfolded with a Nazi armband, the officers indulging themselves accompanied by the music of Nazi marches. It is possible that her sister, Diana (who had secretly married the widowed Mosley in Germany), was also involved in these sessions with the 'Storms' (storm-troopers), though perhaps as a spectator.

Additionally, Unity had become what she herself described as a Jew-hater, befriending Julius Streicher, the Jew baiter and torturer. Her blossoming relationship with Hitler, however, resulted in the gift of a flat but does not appear to have been sexual (he of course was involved with Eva Braun), but this does not seem to have fazed her. Visiting Britain in 1936, she realised how unpopular she had become and over the next few years she was loath to leave Germany. When Britain was confirmed as being at war with Germany in September 1939, Unity shot herself in the head in a Munich park.

Her suicide attempt failed and she was stretchered home, where her damaged health helped her avoid charges, as she seemed to represent no threat to national security. Diana and her husband were less fortunate, being imprisoned from 1940–1943. But the most hated woman in Britain had a quiet ending. In 1948, the bullet in her brain finally killed her – causing a cerebral abscess which brought on meningitis.

O'MALLEY, Grace c.1530–c.1603

The daughter of a County Mayo chieftain and sea captain, Grace was born into a family that had become wealthy through fishing and trading. As a female, she was discouraged from going to sea and there is a legend that she cut off her hair and dressed as a boy, her efforts meaning that she was allowed to sail with her father on overseas trading missions. On one such mission, there is another story that suggests she 'saved' her father from an English pirate who climbed aboard their vessel, by leaping onto the intruder's back.

As young as sixteen, she married the son of another Irish chieftain, a marriage likely to have been a political convenience. However, she learned to control his fleet of ships with considerable skill. Donal-an-Chogaidh O'Flaherty, her hot-tempered husband, was constantly feuding to increase his territory and was mortally wounded in one such skirmish in around 1560, leaving Grace with three young children.

To maintain her family, although Gaelic laws left her in possession of her father's ships, she took to plundering any passing vessels that were unprotected. She built up a fleet of between five and twenty vessels, employing as many as 200 men, attacking shipping on a regular basis around the Irish coast.

There was a much briefer marriage, to Richard Bourke in 1567, which could have been an advantage for both of them in withstanding English invasions. Officially, this lasted only one year, during which she continued to ply her 'trade', but they remained legally married until his death around seventeen years later. In the meantime, she remained based at his home in Rockfleet Castle, in Carraigahowley, Co. Mayo and took the title Lady Bourke when he was knighted in 1581. Their son's birth produced another legend; that he was born on one of her galleys, which was attacked just hours later, but which attack Grace still managed to defend successfully, fresh from labour.

In 1577, she met Sir Henry Sidney, the Lord Deputy of Ireland, who regarded her as a 'notorious woman' but was also impressed with her military prowess. The same year, however, she was arrested after plundering the ancient Irish Kingdom of Desmond, spending two years in prison. She was apparently released by the English who may have hoped she could bring her rebellious husband to heel – a false hope.

Although the couple moved – to Lough Mask Castle near Ballinrobe – after Richard was knighted, Grace moved back to Rockfleet Castle when he died of natural causes in 1583, with 1,000 head of 'cows and mares' and a horde of followers. But the new English governor – Sir Richard Bingham – focused on Grace as a trouble-maker, his brother murdering her eldest son. Not unexpectedly, Grace became an active rebel and was captured and imprisoned and faced the death penalty. But her son-in-law offered himself as hostage in exchange for a promise that she would keep the peace. However, after a period in exile, she joined forces with the King of Spain's Irish allies against England, although there exists a conflicting account of her slaughtering hundreds of Spaniards near Clare Island.

Now seen as a traitor, she was enraged by Bingham's perceived hold over her second son and went back on the attack aided by her youngest son. Bingham retaliated; he plundered her territory and impounded her fleet. Having lost everything, she appealed to Elizabeth I in person in 1593 and again in 1595, assuring her that she would use her strength to defend the Queen. Bingham disagreed with Elizabeth's clemency, continuing to make Grace's life difficult. But after his recall to England, Grace could continue her old career.

As late as 1601, she is still recorded as leading her men against an English warship, thus breaking her promise. She is believed to have died in 1603, a proud and brave adventurer defending her family and her 'rights' to the end, although English rule spread throughout Ireland during her lifetime.

SAPPHO c.625–570 BC

One of the few well known female poets from ancient history, Sappho, thanks to marriage at twenty-one to a prosperous husband, was able to indulge her interest on the Greek island of Lesbos. Her poems, some of which in fact pre-date her marriage, were accompanied by the lyre, for which she also composed the music.

Portrait on vase.

Many of her books of poetry were apparently burned at different periods of history because of the offence they were said to cause the Christian church. Thus, only fragments of her prolific output survive. It is clear that the themes of her work were mostly concerned with love, often interpreted erotically and with the affection aimed mostly at women. This is how the words lesbian and sapphic originated. Christian censors described her in such terms as 'a whore who sang about her own licentiousness'.

While on the one hand she was regarded as the founder of lyric poetry, with Plato referring to her as the tenth Muse, others derided and attacked her sexual preferences. Others excuse the latter, claiming that this was a result of the shortage of men who were at war and/or because she lacked conventional female beauty, making her less likely to attract men.

Although lesbianism in itself does not make her bad, or wicked, the activities of the Academy for Young Girls that Sappho set up is more questionable. Ostensibly, she taught poetry, music and dance, but did it also supply her with vulnerable lovers? Or was she training them to be courtesans?

In Sappho's time, it was not unusual for Greek men to be homosexual (her first male suitor, the poet Alkaios, for example) and the women of Lesbos had as much freedom as modern women in the Western world. There was certainly a very different moral code, with virginity not regarded as a virtue and no prudery, making it difficult for a twenty-first century judgment of any kind.

It was her political views that led to her being exiled for a while to Sicily around the time she met her husband, where there were colonies of Greeks – and this is where it seems she gave birth to her only child, a daughter, Kleis. The locals were said to enjoy lewd entertainment, so Sappho was quite at home there! The husband disappeared (or died?) at some point and she lived as a gay widow, leading the hedonism, until able to return to her native Lesbos.

The young girls who kept her company included Atthis, who became the focus for her poetry, and also for her jealousy. Atthis did not stay faithful and Sappho used her emotions to fuel more poetry. Interestingly, at the age of fifty-five, she became obsessed not with a young woman but with a young, handsome sailor, Phaon, leading to a torrid but brief affair. However, he seems to have fled the island to escape her attentions, leaving her grief-stricken. Sappho pursued him by ship, but seems to have realised at some point that she was making a fool of herself and she is said to have flung herself to death from a cliff-top.

However, Sappho's death, the existence of a husband, her Academy, even her lesbianism, have all been denied by historians over the years. This account gives benefit to some of the doubts that exist. What is true is that she was so renowned in Greece for her poetry that statues were erected in her honour – and that she was a poet of immense talent whose work made her famous then, and still.

TREFUSIS, Violet 1894–1972

Violet was the (probably illegitimate) daughter of Edward VII's mistress, Alice Keppel but their lives went in very different directions with Violet becoming the more obviously outrageous. Her early childhood was understandably privileged, mixing in royal circles, and she was well educated with a flair for languages. In fact, it was at her London girls' school that she met the wealthy Vita Sackville-West who was already having a lesbian affair with Rosamund Grosvenor. Vita and Violet nevertheless shared a childish mutual passion, visiting Italy together in 1908.

In 1912 Vita, however, married the diplomat, Harold Nicolson, who kept his homosexual affairs very discreet. Violet became linked with a couple of bachelors, but the mutual attraction between the two women flared again in 1918 when they began their affair. They wrote poetry, revelled in music and were responsible for a novel using their disguised selves as protagonists. However, Violet's mother persuaded her to marry Denys Trefusis, a Royal Horse Guards officer, although Violet refused to consummate the marriage and continued her affair with Vita. The two women eloped to France in 1920, but their husbands followed in a two-seater plane and managed to initiate a separation, possibly by suggesting that Violet had actually had sex with Denys, which would have infuriated Vita. But they were unable to put a stop to Violet's ardent love letters.

She comforted herself in the arms of the daughter of Isaac Singer, the sewing machine millionaire, rarely meeting up with her husband, who died of tuberculosis in 1929. Winaretta Singer was also married to a homosexual and the relationship between the two women seemed to be similar to Violet's relationship with Vita, in that Violet was the subservient, submissive partner. In the meantime, Violet was writing novels in English and French which had encouraging sales.

Her years in the ambulance service in Britain during the Second World War may have had an influence on her sexual preference, because after that her companions became predominantly male. Vita and Violet did meet up from time to time, but Vita was not impressed with how Violet was ageing. She died – of starvation, due to an inability to digest food – in Italy, at her late mother's villa. Something she once said seems an appropriate epitaph:

Across my life only one word will be written 'waste' – waste of love, waste of talent, waste of enterprise.

WEST, Mae 1893–1980

Mae's parents were as colourful as might be expected; Battling Jack West (a boxer) and a corset model. Born in New York, she was attracted by the stage at a young age and appeared in vaudeville from the age of fourteen as the Baby Vamp. By the age of eighteen, she was on stage with the New York *Folies Bergere* – her first big break; although she returned successfully to vaudeville as a 'singing comedienne' afterwards, which was more suited to her talents.

She acquired her bawdy reputation for sexual innuendo much later, however, not just on stage, but as a writer. It was 1927 when she created a real sensation on Broadway, the year she starred in her play, *Sex*, which she wrote, produced and directed. There were plenty of protests against the play – about a prostitute marrying a rich man – but, not unusually, such protests just aroused more interest. The show was raided after less than forty performances and Mae was charged with obscenity and corrupting the morals of youth. As a result, she was sentenced to ten days in prison and a $500 fine.

Mae West.

She apparently arrived at New York's Welfare Island Prison in a limousine, building on her initial notoriety, and is rumoured to have been allowed to wear silk panties instead of scratchy prison issue and to have dined with the warden and his wife. The inmates were said to have provided her with plenty of material for her vaudeville act. She was released early due to good behaviour, this being, as she was quick to inform journalists, the first time she was ever credited with good behaviour.

As one of the first American female playwrights, many of Mae's subsequent plays were just as controversial. They included *The Pleasure Man* which dealt with homosexuality (and was shut down after one day, with all the cast arrested but later released), *Diamond Lil* which did rather better and established her on and off screen persona and *The Constant Sinner*, shut down after two days. With poor reviews but an enthusiastic following, Hollywood came knocking – albeit at a later age than was usual.

The risqué Thirties comedies she appeared in were ground breaking in their depiction of women and their sexual references. Mae was even allowed to re-write some of her lines in her own inimitable fashion, although she had to battle with the censors. Her first film, *Night After Night*, in 1932, illustrates her skill with the double entendre when a hat check girl compliments her character with the comment, 'Goodness, what beautiful diamonds.' Mae's re-written response was, 'Goodness had nothing to do with it, dearie.'

It took Mae just three years to become the second highest paid individual in the USA, with only William Randolph Hearst, the newspaper magnate, achieving more! By then, the voluptuous actress had been married, briefly, but kept the marriage quiet, re-inventing herself as a feminist. She only made twelve films, but her eccentric, even vulgar, personality – and especially her one-liners – achieved fame well beyond this parameter. Although you might have missed her films, you may know her from the cover of the *Sergeant Pepper's Lonely Hearts Club* album or as the inspiration for Salvador Dali's red sofa!

WOLLSTONECRAFT, Mary 1759–97

Mary is included for diverse and different reasons from other women in this book. True, she had a relationship with a bi-sexual painter and an illegitimate daughter with an adventurer … but it was her thought processes that evoked the bigger outcry, as apparent in her written work.

Mary Wollstonecraft.

She was from a middle class Spitalfields family, her father having inherited a silk weaving business from his father, but showing more interest in alcohol and in bullying than in weaving. This meant that the family – she had six siblings – struggled financially, and moved on to trying out farming for a living, in a number of locations, mainly in Essex. Failing again, this time as a farmer, her father returned the family back to London in 1774 when Mary was fifteen.

Although it was the eldest son who had been formally educated, Mary acquired an impressive stock of knowledge along the way, including several languages. This gave her some independence so that she could progress beyond the traditional eighteenth century occupations for women (needlewoman, companion, governess) to running a girls' school and thence to becoming a professional writer. She did not take the novel-writing route, being more interested in the education and rights of women, facilitated by her new contacts, the 'rational dissenters', who approved of sexual equality. After the publication of *Thoughts on the Education of Daughters*, she was offered a regular column in the *Analytical Review*, becoming the most famous female political writer in Europe.

Although an attractive woman, she preferred to look like an impoverished bohemian with coarse linen garments and black stockings with her hair loose rather than pinned up. Several books later, it was her *A Vindication of the Rights of Woman* that became a bestseller in 1792 (and still sells today). She wrote about women's sexuality for the first time, portrayed marriage as slavery, and also argued 'outrageously' that women were capable of 'reason' – they just needed education.

As for her relationships – after a romantic friendship from a young age with Fanny Blood, which can be interpreted in various ways – these were as unconventional as her writings. Mary became infatuated with the painter Henry Fuseli, a married bi-sexual twenty years her senior, but he would not leave his wife and turned down Mary's suggestion that she join the marital home.

She reacted by moving to Paris in 1792, mixing in bohemian circles and falling for adventurer Gilbert Imlay. Paris was obviously not the best place to be at the time, especially once she fell pregnant; she then followed Imlay to Le Havre, but he was not interested in becoming a family man and was seeing other women, driving Mary to her first suicide attempt with an opium overdose. She actually went against the advice she gave to women, following him to Scandinavia with their baby daughter in 1795, then back to London, but was unable to salvage their relationship. Another suicide attempt – drowning in the Thames – was thwarted by passing watermen.

Enter William Godwin, the philosopher, a meeting of minds which morphed into a passionate affair for several years. Neither of them were interested in marriage, which Mary saw as legal prostitution, again provoking criticism. But when she was pregnant for a second time, the couple did marry – with reservations – in 1797. Sadly, she died when baby Mary (later

Mary Shelley) was eleven days old of 'childbed fever'; septicemia. Even her death was used by critics as 'proof' of the inequality of women.

It was William who sealed her notoriety, writing of her in a biography as leading a 'licentious lifestyle' which resulted in her being described down the years as a 'hyena in petticoats'. But it was her views rather than her lifestyle that were then regarded as scandalous, views now interpreted rather differently.

Select Bibliography

Cordingly, David, *Heroines & Harlots*, Random House, N.Y., 2001.

Donaldson, William, *Brewer's Rogues, Villains & Eccentrics*, Cassell, London, 2002.

Enss, Chris, *Wicked Women*, Rowman & Littlefield, Maryland U.S.A., 2015.

Ewart, Andrew, *The World's Most Wicked Women*, Odhams Books, London, 1964.

Gordon, Dee, *Infamous Essex Women*, The History Press, Slough, 2012.

Linnane, Fergus, *London The Wicked City*, Robson Books, London, 2007.

Love, Andrea, *The Ultimate Celebrity Love Secrets & Scandals Book*, Carlton Books, London, 1998.

Lower, Wendy, *Hitler's Furies*, Chatto & Windus, London, 2013.

Mahon, Elizabeth Kerri, *Scandalous Women*, Penguin Group, N.Y., 2011.

Maine, C.E. *World-Famous Mistresses*, Odhams Books London, 1970.

Nicholas, Margaret, *The World's Wickedest Women*, Octopus Books, London, 1984.

Richardson, Joanna, *The Courtesans*, Weidenfeld & Nicolson, London, 1967.

Robins, Joyce, *Lady Killers*, Chancellor Press, London, 1993.

Skelton, Douglas, *Deadlier than the Male*, Black and White Publishing, Edinburgh, 2003.

Stradling, Jan, *Good Girls Don't Make History*, Pier 9, N.S.W., 2010.

Murder Casebook published by Marshall Cavendish, numerous issues from 1990s.

Select Websites

www.bbc.co.uk
www.biography.com
www.britannica.com
www.britishnewspaperarchive.co.uk
www.capitalpunishmentuk.org
www.crimeandinvestigation.co.uk
www.history.com
www.murderpedia.org
www.notablebiographies.com
www.oldbaileyonline.org
www.oxforddnb.com

Index